• A HISTORY LOVER'S •
GUIDE TO
HOUSTON

• A HISTORY LOVER'S •
GUIDE TO
HOUSTON

TRISTAN SMITH

THE
History
PRESS

Published by The History Press
Charleston, SC
www.historypress.com

Front cover, bottom: Downtown Houston skyline, early twenty-first century. *Carol Highsmith Archive, Library of Congress.*
Front cover, top left: Alabama Theatre, 1977. *Library of Congress.*
Back cover, inset: Foley Brothers Store, early tewntieth century. *Special Collections, University of Houston Libraries.*

First published 2020

Manufactured in the United States

ISBN 9781467144667

Library of Congress Control Number: 2019954233

Notice: The information in this book is true and complete to the best of our knowledge. It is offered without guarantee on the part of the author or The History Press. The author and The History Press disclaim all liability in connection with the use of this book.

For Theo and Max,

You inspire me to preserve the past for your future.

CONTENTS

Acknowledgements   9
Preface   11
Introduction   13

PART I: DOWNTOWN HOUSTON
1. First Ward   23
2. Second Ward   28
3. Third Ward   36
4. Fourth Ward   65
5. Fifth Ward   111
6. Sixth Ward   117

PART II: HOUSTON'S WARDS
1. First Ward   121
2. Second Ward   124
3. Third Ward   130
4. Fourth Ward   142
5. Fifth Ward   151
6. Sixth Ward   155

PART III: OUTSIDE THE WARDS
1. The Heights   163
2. Rice Village   171

CONTENTS

3. River Oaks   176
4. Other Notable Landmarks   185

Bibliography   193
Index   201
About the Author   207

ACKNOWLEDGEMENTS

Since I was young, I liked to explore. I grew up near "the woods," essentially a good-sized wooded area running around a small lake in the neighborhood—big enough to get lost in but not big enough to get truly lost. I am grateful to my parents, Greg and Vicki Smith, for giving me and my brothers the freedom to explore until the porch lights came on.

When I first moved to Houston in 2011, I picked up two books to help guide me as I started work at the Fire Museum. The first was *Historic Photos of Houston* by Betty Trapp Chapman, a renowned independent historian and writer who is one of the go-to people when it comes to Houston history. The other was an edition of Stephen Fox's *Houston Architectural Guide*. This is the *true* guide to Houston's architectural history. Please buy his book and use it to explore Houston's built environment in depth.

I would like to thank Ben Gibson, my editor at The History Press, who has provided guidance, assistance and gentle prodding; and to copyeditor extraordinaire Hayley Behal, for making corrections that only serve to make this book better. Additionally, I'd like to clue you in to a few resources I've found to be golden since moving to Houston. I'd like to point a finger at James Glassman, the Houstorian whose website and social media output on the daily history of Houston is unmatched. Kudos to Robert Kimberly's Sig Byrd archival project. If you read enough Houston history, you'll come across the old column The Stroller by Sigman Byrd, *Houston Press* columnist from 1947 to the mid-1950s; his project brings the city together online. Check it out. Swamplot, an online column about Houston's real estate landscape was a treasure-trove of information on what historic Houston buildings were in peril. Luckily for you, the archives are still around. Also, make it out to Story Sloane's Gallery on Dairy Ashford in west Houston—you won't find a better collection of images or a better storyteller.

Finally, to Jen, thank you for your love and encouragement, I'm definitely "The Luckiest." To Jen, Theo, Max, Grace and Grant, thanks for putting up with me, supporting me, cheering me on and exploring this great city—and beyond—on our "Smanson Adventures."

PREFACE

A *History Lover's Guide to Houston* is an exploration of historic downtown Houston. I moved here in August 2011, from a city trenched firmly in historic preservation, Lawrence, Kansas. This college town of about 100,000 people is home to many historic structures and districts. As I sat on the historic resources commission, I saw firsthand not only the struggles of preserving a community's historic fabric but also the struggles of attempting to grow in it. When I moved to Houston, I encountered a city that had struggled to hold on to its past while traveling at lightspeed to the future, felling numerous stories along the way.

I'm an explorer. I like to discover my city, street by street, neighborhood by neighborhood, building by building. I find adaptive reuse of historic properties fascinating and am amazed by the work people put into the restoration of historic structures. My purpose for this book is to help others explore the historic fabric of downtown Houston. I want others to experience what we have left in the way of historic buildings. While not enough, I think we have a good number of historic buildings to appreciate. I also think that an informed and interested base of people will add to the number of those hoping to save future projects from demolition. We already have amazing work from those at the Greater Houston Preservation Alliance, the Texas Historical Commission, the Heritage Society and the Houston Archaeological and Historic Commission, along with numerous individuals, architects and engineers working to highlight historic preservation efforts in our community. I hope readers of this book will add to that force.

This book is not meant to be a complete listing of all historic structures in Houston, nor is it comprehensive; however, it is a good overview. I'd like for you to read and explore—to take the book with you. I've walked and driven the streets of downtown taking notes, researched the National Register of Historic Places and perused the listings of the city's historic preservation landmarks to collect the buildings in this book.

I hope that you enjoy this book. I hope that you take it and explore downtown Houston. I hope you get involved with the preservation of our community in ways that maybe you hadn't before.

INTRODUCTION

The first Anglo settlers in southeast Texas were members of Stephen F. Austin's Old 300, remaining in Brazoria County, south of present-day Houston, in the 1820s. Working with the Mexican government, Austin had encouraged settlers to come to Texas to colonize the area.

In August 1836, brothers Augustus Allen and John Allen, who arrived in Texas five years prior, purchased six thousand acres of land running along Buffalo Bayou, part of John Austin's (no relation to Stephen) original survey. In November, with land surveyed, they laid out the original town plat, with Main Street running through the center of town. It was located between White Oak and Buffalo Bayous, and the Allen brothers thought that Buffalo Bayou could become an important shipping route between the Gulf Coast and the interior of the new Republic of Texas. Houston contained sixty-two blocks and sixteen streets laid in an off-center grid along the bayou.

The Allens promoted their new town—named for General Sam Houston, cleared the land and began selling parcels, giving little attention to any future development. In fact, some of the earliest accounts of Houston recount the streets and blocks of the new town becoming muddy after rain and pockmarked with tree stumps in the right of way. Reserves were set aside for a courthouse, market house, capitol for the Republic of Texas and, on the southern edge of town, a church and a school. Little other development regulation was established. The town was officially chartered in 1837.

Early residents and visitors to Houston could find emergency accommodations that were hastily built to provide shelter for general life and

The Original Plan of Houston map, an 1869 reproduction of Gail Borden and Moses Lapham's 1836 original commissioned by the Allen brothers. The map shows a city with all roads leading to or away from Buffalo Bayou, the main artery of the heart of Houston. Many of the street names remain the same, with space reserved for a courthouse, churches and schools. *Courtesy of Special Collections, University of Houston Libraries.*

business. Until proper sawmills could be established, most structures were tents or simple log structures. Eventually, these would be replaced with wood frame buildings and then replaced by masonry structures both for stability and to stave off the destructive fires that were common in Houston.

During Houston's first decade, with little established in the way of development regulation, it was common to find residences located directly next to businesses. The city began to expand on all sides, and in 1839, the same year the capital was moved to Austin, Houston was divided into four wards for voting and city management purposes. These wards came together at the axis of Main and Congress Streets.

The first economic boom came in the 1850s, resulting directly from the construction of the Houston and Texas Central Railway. The city had become a major southern shipping center and a hub for rail activity. With this growth, the value of real estate increased, quickly outgrowing the value for residential use. Neighborhoods started being established on the farther reaches of the city, including one to the east called Quality Hill.

A daguerreotype of Sam Houston taken some time between 1848 and 1850 by famed photographer Matthew Brady. His legacy includes service in the War of 1812 and leading the Texian Army to victory at the Battle of San Jacinto, while his political career lists service as Republic of Texas president (1836–38 and 1841–44), U.S. House of Representatives for Tennessee 1823–27 and Texas 1839–41), Senate (1846–59) and governor of Tennessee (1827–29) and Texas (1859–61). *Courtesy of Library of Congress.*

Following the Civil War, Houston continued to grow, and the ongoing extension of rail service throughout Texas resulted in increased access for Houston merchants and an influx of money. City leaders followed with civic improvements, finishing the Harris County Courthouse and constructing a permanent city hall and market house. Neighboring buildings for new or growing businesses followed suit around Market Square in the late 1860s and into the 1870s. As technology advanced, so did the need for businesses and developers to make their buildings stand out. New construction methods and materials, along with daring engineers and architects, brought a new wave of buildings, growing higher along the skyline as Houston approached and then passed the turn of the century.

The Allen brothers were prescient—thinking their new town would benefit from the location of the bayou and its proximity to the Gulf turned out to be correct. With the construction of the Houston Ship Channel and

By 1873, Houston had become a busy center of commerce. Its business district was vibrant, expanding and becoming well known throughout the country as an important port. The nearby island of Galveston would continue to overshadow its neighbor until the devastating hurricane of 1900 caused that focus to shift inland to Houston. *Courtesy of Library of Congress.*

The Turning Basin in the Port of Houston, seen here with the cruiser *Houston*, is home to several oil refineries and docks for Houston's vast network of industrial companies. The port is one of the busiest seaports in the United States. *Courtesy of National Archives.*

Port of Houston, the city grew rapidly, easily overtaking the once-larger island town of Galveston and soon surpassing all other Texas cities in size. This growth brought more money and more growth, enabling developers to bring in architects from around the country.

A prominent figure during the early twentieth century was city leader and businessman Jesse Jones. Many Houston architects called Jones either a direct benefactor or, at the very least, an influencer of their projects. The firm of Mauran, Russell, and Crowell from St. Louis could mark seven Houston buildings associated with Jones. By 1913, the year the concrete Main Street viaduct was constructed to cross Buffalo Bayou, Houston's building boom went quiet.

This explosion of growth continued to push downtown business boundaries away from the core surrounding Market Square, the original heart of the city. As the city grew, the neighboring residences on the edges of town began to move farther away and were swallowed up by civic and commercial enterprises. Much of Quality Hill was eliminated with the

Jesse Jones (*left*) takes oath as federal loan administrator on July 17, 1939. Jones, a politician and entrepreneur from Houston, went on to serve as the United States secretary of Commerce from 1940 until 1945. His influence in Houston, however, stretched throughout most of his adult life. His activity would be felt architecturally, in the commercial sector, in the media and a variety of civic and political avenues. Houston likely would not be the metropolis it is today without his influence. *Courtesy of Library of Congress.*

construction of Union Station, and residences on the south side of downtown would continue to push in the southward direction, forming what is today the Midtown District.

After World War I, Houston saw another period of growth, this time with most of the projects located outside the Market Square District, an area that was content in its stability. Buildings continued to be built taller and taller. Houston's skyline changed at what seemed to be an annual rate. By the beginning of the Great Depression, the civic center and the heart of downtown's commerce district had moved beyond Market Square. The 1904 city hall was replaced by a newer building and was converted to a bus station.

During the 1950s, downtown buildings that were considered old and unable to conform to modern necessities began to fall, many making way for parking lots while others were modernized and converted into office buildings. In 1960, the old 1904 city hall and the neighboring market building burned.

By the end of the 1960s, downtown had expanded exponentially since its founding, and a new highway system, leading into and out of downtown, had been started. This would eventually frame a boundary for the downtown district, with major highways or federal interstates running around the city. Market Square and Allen's Landing were converted into parks during the 1960s and 1970s, joining Sam Houston Park downtown.

Houston has always been a city of growth, of looking to the future rather than to the past. One organization in particular has taken up the mantle of historic preservation. The Greater Houston Preservation Alliance was incorporated in 1978, and, with neighborhood representatives in 1995, convinced Mayor Bob Lanier that the city needed to protect its historic resources. This work resulted in the passage of the city's first historic preservation ordinance. In 2012, it rebranded to Preservation Houston and

This aerial photo of downtown Houston was taken in 1947. Just above the cloud shadow, near the center of the photograph, is the ribbon of Buffalo Bayou that meanders north of downtown. *Courtesy of National Archives.*

has continued to lead the charge for historic preservation in Houston. Not all buildings can be saved, but through the efforts of concerned individuals and organizations such as this, at least there is a louder voice calling for discussion and activism.

I have divided this book up using Houston's ward system. While they were officially in use for only a short time, they've continued to be used locally as descriptors. For the downtown section, I've broken the area into the six wards of Houston, using the Main and Congress axis as the common connector with boundaries stretching out from there. Since Houston no longer uses the ward system, and because of the immense changes that have taken place downtown over the past 175-plus years, I've forgone the descriptions of the various wards until we leave downtown. You'll find those introducing the historic sites later on, as they have retained some of their identity primarily away from the confines of the city center.

PART I
DOWNTOWN HOUSTON

FIRST WARD

JEFFERSON DAVIS HOSPITAL

1101 Elder Street

Originally the site of a municipal cemetery and burial grounds for the City of Houston, this is where more than six thousand Confederate army soldiers, former slaves and city officials were laid to rest, including thousands of yellow fever and cholera victims. The cemetery operated from 1840 until 1879, with some family burials continuing into the 1890s before falling into disuse. In the 1920s, the city used the site for the new Jefferson Davis Hospital.

The basement was placed above ground when construction began in 1924, and while many graves were relocated, it has since been discovered that there was no wholesale removal of the remains. The hospital served Houston until 1938 and then was used for a variety of purposes before being abandoned in the 1980s.

Today, the building is listed as a city landmark by the City of Houston Archeological and Historical Commission and has been transformed into a series of artist lofts and residential housing units known as the Elder Street Artist Lofts. Restoration was completed in 2005. A remaining unrestored portion was destroyed in a 2013 fire, and the two-floor nurses' quarters were demolished after storm damage in 2017.

Now the Elder Street Artists' Lofts, the Jefferson Davis Hospital opened to patients in 1925. Its stigma as a "haunted property" rose from its construction over the site of the former municipal cemetery and burial grounds. Thousands of Confederate States army soldiers, former slaves, yellow fever and cholera victims and city officials were laid to rest here until the mid-1890s. *Author's collection.*

TENNISON HOTEL

110 Bagby Street

Vinegar Hill, a rough area of old Houston, sat on some of the most profitable land in town. The city cleaned the area in 1881 to make way for improvements and expansion for the Houston and Texas Central Railway. Vinegar Hill's reputation gradually changed until it mostly consisted of factories and stores and became home, in 1922, to Henry Booker "H.B." Tennison's new eponymous hotel.

Sitting across the street from Southern Pacific's Grand Central Station, the red-brick Tennison climbed seven stories atop a limestone base, featured 110 rooms and was marked by its green Tennison flag. When rail traffic dwindled and Grand Central Station was demolished, the hotel's demand declined, until it closed for good in 1972. In 2007, it was renovated as loft apartments.

At the turn of the century, Houston's Grand Central Station depot was an active hub of activity for both commercial and leisure travel, referred to as "where 17 railroads meet the sea." Today, only a small Amtrak station, at 902 Washington, casts a shadow of the city's former rail station prominence. *Courtesy of Special Collections, University of Houston Libraries.*

MERCHANTS AND MANUFACTURERS BUILDING

1 Main Street

Overlooking downtown, above Allen's Landing at the confluence of Buffalo and White Oak Bayous, the Merchants and Manufacturers Building was built where rail, water and road transportation intersected in the 1920s. The eleven-story Art Deco/Art Noveau building covers four acres and is built of reinforced concrete. It handled rail traffic through its interior and featured a six-story breezeway that helped cool the building. The lower level contained a three-hundred-car parking garage with fourteen miles of floor space above that held offices and retail outlets. Construction was completed in 1930, but within four years, the developers were bankrupt, and the project fell apart.

The sprawling structure was purchased in 1968 by South Texas Junior College, which merged into the University of Houston system in 1974.

The Merchant's and Manufacturer's Building, commonly known as the M & M Building, today serves as a primary structure on the campus of the University of Houston–Downtown. At the time of its construction, in 1930, it was Houston's largest building, featuring fourteen miles of floor space. *Author's collection.*

Today, light rail runs in front of the building, connecting the campus to Rice University, NRG Park, the Museum District, Texas Medical Center and the rest of downtown.

FRANKLIN STREET BRIDGE/DONNELLAN CRYPT

Franklin Street and Buffalo Bayou

Spanning 350 feet over Buffalo Bayou, this stringer bridge was constructed in 1914, though a wooden footbridge appeared here as early as 1885. Below, along the banks of the bayou, was the Donnellan Crypt. Prior to the Civil War, this land was part of the Donnellan settlement. The crypt contained the bodies of patriarch Timothy; his wife, Emily; and their son, Henry, who, according to local lore, found a live Civil War cannonball in 1867. Henry and his friend Charles Ritchey attempted to defuse the detonator cap, causing it to explode, killing them both. In 1903, the bodies were moved to Glenwood Cemetery. The crypt remained and was used to store ordnance during World War I and as support for a new bridge in 1914. Rehabilitated in 1998, it continues to handle traffic, seeing nearly fifteen thousand vehicles daily.

2

SECOND WARD

FROST TOWN/JAMES BUTE PARK

512 McKee Street

While the Allen brothers are credited with founding Houston, the area's first settlement was started by a group of German farmers in the 1820s near the confluence of White Oak and Buffalo Bayous. By 1839, the area had become Frost Town, a thriving community with a post office, school, volunteer fire department, brewery and several places of worship. However, it's neighbor, Houston, took the lead in growth. By the late 1880s, only a few old wood-frame houses remained, and civic improvements continued to dismantle Frost Town. By 1990, only six homes remained, and those were demolished to make way for freeway expansion, leaving Race Street as the only remnant. Today, it is the site of James Bute Park, named after the owner and founder of the Bute Paint Company, a leading contributor to the city's development.

FIRST NATIONAL BANK

201 Main Street

This block-long Beaux-Arts building, constructed in 1905, was home to Houston's first chartered bank, which was established in 1866. Standing at seven stories, it was the city's first steel-framed building and, at the time, Houston's tallest. It was the first Houston building designed by the architectural firm of Sanguinet and Staats.

The L-shaped building, which is ornately decorated inside and out, housed First National Bank facilities on the first floor and basement, with leased office space above. In 1908, the building doubled in size, with additional expansions coming in 1911 and 1925. After First National Bank merged with City National Bank in 1956, new tenants moved in. Developers purchased the building in the 1990s and converted the building into the Franklin Lofts, restoring the banking hall as an event space.

SUNSET COFFEE BUILDING

1019 Commerce Street

The 1910 Sunset Coffee Building is one of the few industrial buildings still located directly on Buffalo Bayou. With three floors above ground and one below, this brick low-rise building was built as an annex to the 1880's W.D. Cleveland and Son's wholesale grocer supply building. Both were located at the foot of Main Street, processing goods as they came into port.

The Sunset Coffee Building is one of the few remaining industrial buildings on Buffalo Bayou, serving originally as a coffee roasting company. Buffalo Bayou Partnership has since purchased and renovated the building to serve as its headquarters, and it includes an outdoor plaza. *Author's collection.*

The building closed in the 1920s, remaining vacant for nearly forty years before local artist David Adickes purchased it in the 1960s and operated Love Street Light Circus and Feel Good Machine on the top floor until 1971. The building then sat vacant until 2003, when Buffalo Bayou Partnership (BBP) purchased it, renovating it for use as offices and a recreation and cultural center and adding a plaza on an adjacent lot. Reconstruction plans took bayou flooding into account with integrated drains and strategically located elevator stops. The ground floor housed an exhibit displaying memorabilia from the building's history.

ALLEN'S LANDING

1001 Commerce Street

Near here, on August 30, 1836, brothers Augustus Chapman and John Kirby Allen stepped ashore and claimed the location as their own. The steamer *Laura* began docking at the new port the following year, and just a few months later, the City of Houston was incorporated.

Officially recognized as the birthplace of Houston, Allen's Landing was advertised as the head of navigation on the bayou and served as Houston's first wharf. While the moniker is more recent, its location was crucial in establishing Houston's prominence for decades to come, sitting at the bayou's confluence with White Oak Bayou, another major tributary. It was named a port in 1841. *Author's collection.*

The landing, a natural turning basin, originally served as a dock for Houston real estate development, hosting numerous oceangoing ships, steamers and sailing vessels that loaded from its wharves. The city officially established the port in June 1841. Then in 1910, federal funding paid for the dredging of a ship channel from the Gulf to the present turning basin, located four miles east of this location.

Dedicated as Allen's Landing Memorial Park in 1967, the site has been improved and developed over the years and serves as a downtown attraction.

TEXAS PACKING COMPANY BUILDING

1119 Commerce Street

Built in 1924, this building, designed by Joseph Finger, was owned and occupied by S.J. San Angelo's Meat Packing plant well into the 1980s. Standing two stories above and two stories below ground, it is typical of buildings constructed in an industrial vernacular style in 1920s Houston. The exposed concrete frame is infilled with red brick and includes a loading dock spanning the length of its Commerce Street façade. Most recently, it has served as home to a bail bonds business and a restaurant.

PALACE HOTEL

216 LaBranch Street

The three-story Palace Hotel is one of only two surviving Romanesque Revival buildings downtown. Built in 1903, the hotel went by a variety of names and consisted of furnished rooms and a communal bath and was operated primarily by women. Ground-floor tenants have included druggists, shoemakers, real estate enterprises, dry goods merchants and several cafés. In 1924, a hotel annex expanded operations to the west, and in 1927, an awning and plate glass storefront was added. The ground floor underwent reconfiguration into office space, and by 1957, the second and third floors had been completely remodeled, with four baths added to each floor.

A bail bond company operated out of the ground floor though the early 2000s. A partnership between Harris County and Palace Partners resulted in the building's rehabilitation in 2005 and included a storefront restoration, brickwork repointing and repairs to cast stone.

ELLER WAGON WORKS/PITTSBURGH PLATE GLASS BUILDING

101 Crawford Street

Frank Eller, a local blacksmith, and his son, Homer, built a strong business manufacturing a variety of wagons, carriages, trucks and trimming in Houston. At the turn of the twentieth century, they began to offer automobile repair, painting and trimming as a specialty. In 1909, they constructed a new three-story, brown brick Victorian building for their burgeoning business. When they left, Texas Wagon Works moved in and stayed until 1920, when Pittsburgh Plate Glass Company (PPG) acquired it.

PPG, which still operates, offers plate and window glass, mirrors, paints, varnishes, brushes, roofing and more. In 1920, PPG added a second

The former home of Eller Wagon Works was renovated in 2004 to house art studios, commercial studios and residential lofts. Remnants of its original purpose are still evident throughout the building today. *Author's collection.*

three-story structure on the south side. Following PPG's departure in the late 1990s, the complex was converted into artist lofts, apartments and a disabled-adults day service. This building was condemned in 2004 but has since been renovated and redeveloped as residential lofts and office and artist gallery space.

PURSE BUILDING

1701 Commerce

Emblazoned with the Purse & Company name on its exterior façade, this three-story, red brick, box-style building is now home to artist studios. Built in 1927 as a furniture warehouse for J.L. Jones, this flat building features a mechanical "penthouse" as its only outstanding feature.

J.W. Northrup, better known for the American Georgian–style homes he designed in River Oaks and the South End, designed this warehouse building and many others for Jones in the 1920s. Most recently, the building contained artist studio spaces, exhibition space on the first floor and smaller exhibition spaces on the other two floors.

The Purse Building originally housed a furniture warehouse and has most recently been the home to artists' studios and exhibition space. *Author's collection.*

NATIONAL BISCUIT COMPANY BUILDING

15 North Chenevert

The National Biscuit Company Building (a.k.a. Nabisco) is one of the few downtown factories remaining today. Starting with a small, three-story production plant building in 1902, the company expanded in 1910 with this five-story southwest regional headquarters for baking, packing and shipping.

This steel-framed brick building features Gothic-style doors and windows set behind wrought-iron gates. Loading docks, roll-up doors and freight elevators run along Chenevert, while the roof features a brick water tower, cistern and an enclosed fire escape tower. Five large ovens once filled the fourth and fifth floors, with a mixing room also on the fifth.

Following World War II, Nabisco moved out and wholesale furniture company Purse & Company, repurposing it for its needs. A concrete warehouse was added to the property in 1969. When Purse & Company moved out in 1982, the building sat vacant until its renovation into loft apartments.

The National Biscuit Company constructed this building for its Houston operations. Placed on the National Register of Historic Places in 1998, it has since been converted into apartment space as City View Lofts. *Author's collection.*

WESTERN ELECTRIC COMPANY BUILDING

100 Jackson Street

Starting in Chicago in the 1870s, Western Electric Company served as a telegraph equipment manufacturer for Western Union. By the time of its Houston debut in 1913, it had been acquired by Bell Telephone and sold everything from lamps to washing machines. By the 1920s, it supplied nearly 90 percent of all telephone equipment in the United States.

Western Electric moved into this new three-story warehouse in 1917. It was one of the earliest in Houston to feature wide, industrial-type metal frame windows. A one-story addition was later constructed on the south side. Western Electric vacated the building in 1926, and International Harvesters moved in, staying until 1935 and selling engines, trucks and farm machinery.

A line of other companies followed: Grocers Supply Company, Peaslee Gualbert Paint and Varnish Company, Wilson Stationery and Printing, Keith Refrigeration and Adsco Line Products, until the building was condemned in the early 2000s. It has undergone renovation since, keeping the hardwood floors intact, freight elevator operational and exposed wood beams and columns in their original condition. It is home to architectural offices, art studios and loft spaces.

3
THIRD WARD

HOUSTON FIRE DEPARTMENT CENTRAL STATION

1300 Preston

Built in 1924, Houston's Central Police and Fire Headquarters on Preston replaced the department's 1924 onion-domed central station that was located at Texas and San Jacinto Streets. Made of brick and stone, this five-story fire station features a Caroline Street entrance with bays leading onto Preston. Fire department administrative offices and dormitories were located on the second floor, and the Houston Police Department (HPD) headquarters occupied the next three floors, with fire alarm services in the penthouse.

In 1940, fire alarm services outgrew the space and moved to a dedicated location at Bagby and Lamar, while HPD got its new headquarters in 1952. Across the street, at Preston and Austin, stood the Houston Fire Department Training Academy. Built as an annex in 1928, it was used until November 1969, when a new training facility opened near Hobby Airport. That same year, a new multistory building was constructed at 410 Bagby for the fire department headquarters and arson and fire prevention offices. The building has been repurposed, hosting jury duty and serving as a Harris County courthouse annex. While little of the exterior on the building has changed, one may not notice that it once was a fire station, save for the bricked-over apparatus bay doors.

NATIONAL CASH REGISTER BUILDING

515 Caroline Street

John Henry Patterson bought the rights of the cash register invention in 1884 and, with his brother, bought out the manufacturing company as well, renaming it the National Cash Register Company. The business grew slowly before becoming one of the largest public offerings by 1925. Arriving in Houston in 1911, National Cash Register occupied two buildings before constructing this two-story concrete and stucco showroom in 1929. Its Italian Renaissance Revival style is unique in Houston.

Patterson promoted progressive working conditions: more glass for better light and ventilation, indoor bathrooms and showers and a ventilation system for clean air. He also offered coffee and soup at lunch, maintained a doctor's office on the premises and offered exercise breaks and chairs for machine operators.

The company operated this showroom until 1943 when it moved to new offices on Fannin. The company still exists, though it was bought by AT&T before spinning off again. This building remains close to its original image and now houses law offices.

SACRED HEART CHURCH

1111 Pierce

The Sacred Heart parish was established in 1896 to serve the city's growing Catholic population. The three-story church opened in 1912, with temporary structures used for services, classes and the rectory in the interim. As the congregation grew, newer buildings replaced older buildings that were then repurposed for other uses. By the beginning of the twenty-first century, the archdiocese had outgrown its complex and decided to build a new Co-Cathedral of the Sacred Heart, which was completed in 2008.

It purchased the adjacent Federal Reserve Bank Building, which became the Cathedral Centre, replacing the 1922 Sacred Heart School building. Calls from preservations and parishioners temporarily halted plans to demolish the historic buildings, which have since been listed by Preservation Texas and Greater Houston Preservation Alliance as some of Texas's Most Endangered Historic Places.

TEXAS STATE HOTEL

720 Fannin Street

Construction began in 1926 with hopes of having the Texas State Hotel ready for the 1928 Democratic National Convention. Nearly three years later, Jesse Jones purchased the building with its interior still incomplete.

The sixteen-story building finally opened its doors in the spring of 1929 and was considered one of the finest in downtown. The exterior is adorned with a variety of coats of arms, glyphs, scrolls, urns and a frieze containing fleur-de-lys, while inside, the lobby features a marble staircase, a ballroom, a formal dining room and a banquet kitchen.

The hotel underwent significant remodeling during the 1960s, which included redecoration and a reconfiguring of rooms. After sitting empty for fifteen years, the building was sold, and restoration work undid much of the 1960s remodel. The exterior was cleaned and restored, and a three-part storefront was constructed before it opened in 2005 as Club Quarters Hotel.

TAMBORELLO BUILDING

1901 Milam

Opening in 1930, this two-story building originally served as the car dealership for J.S. Tamborello. The tan brick façade is embellished with Spanish-themed details and a roof of red tile. In 2001, the Houston Fire Department moved its firefighters, EMTs and other personnel and equipment from Stations 1 and 8 into this building as a temporary station. Station 8, which had been in a series of building on that site since 1895, was demolished to make way for the Toyota Center, while Station 1, at 410 Bagby, was completely rebuilt and repurposed for use as the downtown aquarium. A new Station 8, with the combined crews, opened at 1919 Louisiana in 2008, and this building was renovated in 2014, although little of its exterior appearance has changed.

TEXAS COMPANY BUILDING

1111 Rusk/720 Jacinto

Texas Fuel Company, later the Texas Company and ultimately Texaco, moved its offices to various Houston buildings during its infancy. By 1913, it had grown into a $60 million company, necessitating one central headquarters. Founding partner Joseph Cullinan purchased a site at the corner of Rusk and San Jacinto, then part of a flourishing residential area, for the new building.

This thirteen-story steel-framed building was finished in 1915 and covered the entire block. It features a second-story balcony, a variety of columns, large arched windows, multiple decorations and a number of Texas Company embellishments, such as initials and the Texaco Star. Expansions came in 1936 and then there was a sixteen-story addition in 1958, and a parking annex was added in 1975, essentially obliterating the interior design along the way. After sitting vacant for about seven years, the building was converted into loft apartments called the Star.

SISTERS OF CHARITY PARK

1404 St. Joseph Parkway

In 1866, the three founding sisters of St. Mary's arrived in Galveston and were taken to the Ursuline convent because their new convent and hospital were under construction. They moved into the new convent in 1867, starting the charity hospital, St. Mary's Infirmary, that April. Over the years, the hospital led Houston's fight against a yellow fever epidemic and suffered a massive fire that killed two sisters but spared all of the patients.

The park, dedicated to the sisters' long history and service to Houston's community, includes carved crosses, intricately carved stonework, a rocky waterfall, exterior views of the adjacent building's stained-glass windows, statuary and abundant landscaping and a labyrinth. Located on the southern edge of downtown, the Sisters of Charity Park is maintained by Christus St. Joseph Hospital, a successor of the original St. Joseph Hospital system established by the Sisters of Charity of the Incarnate Word.

ST. JOSEPH HOSPITAL CONVENT AND CHAPEL

1903 Crawford Street

St. Joseph Infirmary, established in 1887 by the Sisters of Charity of the Incarnate Word, was started in a small frame structure at Caroline and Franklin and evolved into the St. Joseph Medical Center, Houston's oldest hospital. In 1888, the hospital partnered with Harris County to care for the city's indigent patients. A larger brick facility opened in 1894 but was destroyed a few months later by a fire that killed two nuns.

Its replacement opened in 1905, followed by a nursing annex in 1919, a maternity building in 1938 and then another annex and the current brick convent and dormitory in 1940. The convent features a garden, a chapel, a large fifth-floor balcony and an enclosed courtyard with a pool and diving board. Inside the chapel, tall arched windows feature ornate stained-glass windows and marble staircases. Until Texas Medical Center, St. Joseph's was the largest hospital in Houston, and it continues to operate. The convent building sits empty.

PEACOCK AND PLAZA COURT APARTMENTS

1414–1416 Austin Street

Attempting to capitalize on a Houston building boom, this apartment complex was constructed on the southeast outskirts of downtown. The Peacock Apartments opened in 1924 and the adjacent Plaza Court in 1925. Both Mission-style buildings are two-story, U-shaped structures with narrow courtyards. They are almost identical. The Peacock features windows shielded by green and white striped metal awnings and painted Spanish tiles depicting a peacock and its name.

The Plaza's original tile decoration is gone, replaced with a decorative stone infill with a carved floral design and its name that was added around 2007. The complex recently underwent renovations but continues to house thirty-two apartments with three rooms each. Until recently, many of the original appliances and Murphy beds were still in use. The apartment building, one of few surviving from the era, continue to serve as some of the most inexpensive apartments in downtown Houston.

The two-building complex of the Plaza and Peacock apartments was constructed in 1926 and 1940 by Houston architect Lenard Gabert. Following a one-person ownership for the past eight decades, the complex has recently undergone upgrades and modernization. *Author's collection.*

ROOT MEMORIAL SQUARE

1400 Clay Street

One of downtown's earliest parks, this land was donated to the City of Houston in 1923 by the descendants of Alexander Porter Root and his wife, Laura. Root was born in 1840 in Delaware but made 1410 Clay Avenue his home in this residential area of downtown, then located outside the southeastern edge of the business district. He died in 1908 and is buried with his wife at Houston's Glenwood Cemetery.

Today, Root Memorial Square sits across La Branch Street from the Toyota Center, home of the Houston Rockets. Renovations in 2005 added new sidewalks, an art feature depicting the once-grand Victorian residences that sat nearby, an irrigation system, a basketball court, a shade pavilion, a fountain and improved lighting.

MASONIC TEMPLE

1401–1407 Fannin Street

This 1923 building originally served as a branch home to the Grand Lodge of Texas. Standing at three stories, with its name etched into its façade, this temple was designed by Alfred Charles Finn and was constructed by Mason Tom Tellepson's eponymous construction company. In 2009, a time capsule was discovered in an exterior wall. Inside were items synonymous with the Masons, such as kilts, fezzes, dues cards, faded scraps of papers and a copy of the *Houston Dispatch* from the laying of the cornerstone. The building is currently occupied by Medallion Oil Company.

SAKOWITZ DEPARTMENT STORE

1111 Main

Founded in 1902 in Galveston by brothers Tobias and Simon Sakowitz, the Sakowitz Department Store moved to downtown Houston in 1917. This 1951, marble-clad, Art Moderne–style building was to be the company's flagship store. This was the third location and was directly across the street from its competitor, Foley's. It included a fifth-floor sky terrace dining room, hand-painted murals, wall display niches and 122 private fitting rooms.

By the late 1980s, Sakowitz had expanded to thirteen locations, ten of which were in Texas, but the company was sold, and the stores closed by 1990. In 1998, the old flagship store was converted to a parking garage.

CITY NATIONAL BANK

1001 McKinney Avenue

This Art Moderne, fifteen-story office building was one of downtown's first post–World War II projects. Plans began in 1939, but World War II delayed completion until 1947. Original tenants included Braniff International, Humble Oil, Philips Petroleum, Monstanto Chemical and radio station KPRC's control room and transmitting tower. The building used the new Robertson cellular flooring, which eliminated the need for ceiling beams and removed conduits running across walls, ceilings or floors. The building featured a three-story banking room, bank offices and Corrigan's Jewelry Store. The upper floors contained commercial office space and mechanical systems, and the basement had enormous bank vaults.

The twenty-three-story City National Bank building was designed by Alfred C. Finn. It has recently undergone extensive renovations and visitors are greeted by a redesigned two-story lobby. Among some of its well-known tenants were national companies such as DuPont, Braniff, Monsanto,and Humble Oil (later Exxon). Local radio station KPRC transmitted from the twenty-third floor. *Author's collection.*

A 1956 merger with First National Bank resulted in a new building in 1961. This building has seen no real structural and few design modifications since its construction, but the "City National Bank" sign above the entrances on Main and McKinney has been removed.

KIRBY BUILDING

917 Main Street

The eleven-story Kirby Building was built in 1926 for lumber baron John Henry Kirby but is best known as home to the Palais Royal department store. It also served as home to the Kirby Theater until the 1950s. The storefront and accompanying awning stretched along the ground floor, but no other ornamentation was featured until a band that sits above the ninth-story windows. Above that band, a diamond pattern features two figures flanking an arched center pediment with "Kirby Lumber Company" centered in between. When the theater was still housed here, a "KIRBY" marquee was featured on the side of the building, running above the second floor to the bottom of the seventh.

In 1947, the building was remodeled inside and out to become the Fashion, an upscale women's clothing store. The Fashion eventually grew and occupied much of the building. In 1955, Neiman Marcus merged with the Fashion and opened its downtown branch here—the first of its stores outside Dallas. It operated in this location until 1969 when it moved to the new Galleria shopping mall. Today, the Kirby Building houses the Kirby Lofts and a CVS.

THE SMART SHOP

905 Main Street

The Wexner Brothers entered the Houston market in the 1930s, leasing the shoe department at the Fashion. When the Fashion was bought by Neiman Marcus, which ran its own shoe department, the Wexners moved the shoe operation to another upscale women's specialty store, the Smart Shop.

This 1928 Art Deco building rises five stories tall with a long retail façade on the ground floor topped by two-story windows. The façade was

Originally constructed for Jesse Jones in 1929, Monsignor Albert Beck founded Holy Cross Chapel in the basement of this building in 1982 and purchased the structure in 2001. *Author's collection.*

updated in 1965 by San Jacinto Savings with a slipcover mosaic of the San Jacinto Monument. Since 1982, the Holy Cross Chapel has operated here. Reconstruction in 2003 brought the exterior back to its original appearance, using the original blueprints as a guide. In 2009, the church renovated the second floor, adding a bookstore, conference and meeting rooms, offices and a kitchen.

MELROSE BUILDING

1121 Walker

This skyscraper introduced the sleek Modernist International style to Houston's skyline in 1952. Architecture firm Lloyd and Morgan designed this twenty-one-story building after receiving the freedom to use the most modern materials and techniques to garner immediate attention. The design was used as a vehicle to engage a national discussion on modern office architecture. Interesting features include its asymmetrical design, lightweight concrete construction and cantilevered cast-concrete eyebrows shielding its windows.

Tenants have included dental supply companies, language schools, Texas Pipeline Company, Texaco's South Texas Division and Shell Oil, but by the end of the 1960s, it sat mostly vacant. A 1971 remodel brought in new tenants but was abandoned again in the 1980s for more than two decades. Starwood Hotels and Resorts purchased and renovated the building in 2015, and it is now the high-end European-style hotel Le Meridien, featuring a restored façade and original color scheme.

STOWERS BUILDING

820 Fannin Street

George Arthur Stowers started his furniture business in 1887 at the age of seventeen, eventually operating stores throughout Texas, Alabama and Tennessee, with the headquarters in San Antonio. His first store in Houston opened in 1901 and moved into this building, referred to as "The Big White Store," in 1913.

The ten-story building is a remnant of Houston's early skyscraper exploration. The floorplan featured a two-floor retail showroom with workshops above. Stowers changed its marketing demographic by 1945, looking toward a higher-end customer base. However, by 1966, the store on Fannin closed and moved outside of downtown. The building sold to Gordon's Jewelers, which by 1974, was its last major tenant. Renovations to the building in 2005 altered the building dramatically. In late 2016, Aloft Hotel opened in the building with even more extensive restoration.

UNITED STATES CUSTOMS HOUSE BUILDING

701 San Jacinto

With a new ship channel, nearby oil discovery and fallout from the 1900 hurricane, businesses began settling in Houston rather than Galveston, and demand for improved federal services was high. The Treasury Department's supervising architect, James Knox Taylor, prepared plans for a building housing the federal district court, a post office and additional federal offices, and in 1911, the three-story Customs House opened. Constructed of limestone, brick and granite, it resembles many other federal buildings that Knox designed. Stone steps lead to main entry doors on the west and inside to a central two-story courtroom.

A large addition came in 1931, housing additional federal offices with one-story wings extending to the north and south and four-story elements at the southeast and northeast corners—all connected by a one-story mail room and platform. The courthouse and post office continued to operate in the building until 1962 when new facilities were built. Today, it serves as part of the Harris County Sheriff's office and jail, military recruiting and processing station and USPS station.

M.E. FOSTER BUILDING

715–723 Main Street

The ten-story Houston Bar Center Building started as the M.E. Foster Building and is connected to a single-story building on the northwest that once housed the Zoe and Capitol Theater. The neighboring Gulf Building went up in 1915 and was joined internally to the others in 1929.

The building was originally named for Marcellus Elliot Foster, a former *Houston Post* managing editor and early investor in the Spindletop oil field. Foster had recently founded and was president of the *Houston Chronicle*. Some of the higher-profile tenants included the Great Southern Life Insurance Company, Humble Oil and Refining Company, Gulf Production Company and the first office for the Houston-based international Vinson and Elkins. Other smaller tenants, many related to the oil and gas industry, occupied what space remained.

In 1966, to stay competitive, the building was modernized and combined with the pre-1929 Gulf Building, the Gulf Building annex and the Rusk Building to become the Houston Bar Center. The building was stripped of its ornamentation inside and out and its façade was covered with a bronze-colored, reflective glass curtain wall. It has since been redesigned as lofts and now serves as a hotel. That slipcover eventually met a fifty-year historic threshold, and due to this 1960s remodeling, the Texas Historical Commission recommended its rehabilitation. This was the first time that a slipcover was intentionally preserved in the state.

S.H. KRESS & CO. BUILDING

705 Main Street

Samuel Henry Kress opened his first five-and-dime store in Memphis in 1896 and expanded to five states by 1900. S.H. Kress & Company was different than many early twentieth-century chain retail stores. The company built its own stores with an in-house architecture team, thus allowing for consistency regardless of location.

Covered almost entirely in terra-cotta, this was one of the largest buildings the Kress Department Store company built and was one of the few to incorporate professional offices. A 1983 renovation removed the Kress signage and much of the architectural features unique to the company. *Courtesy of National Archives.*

This was Kress's largest store until a New York City flagship was built in 1913. The eight-story store included typical Kress elements such as a plate glass storefront that curved in toward a recessed entrance, prismatic glass transoms and branded signage and logos. The adjacent two-story brick Gas Building (1910) to the east became an annex in 1947 and then was expanded by two stories. A full redesign came in 1952 and 1953, including a concealed parking section. Kress ceased operations in 1980, and this location was converted into an office building. Renovations in 1983 included alterations to the arched auto entry and storefronts, as well as some exterior alterations and Kress's abundant signage. The building has since been converted into the St. Germain Lofts with retail operations on the ground floor.

SOUTHWESTERN BELL CAPITAL MAIN OFFICE BUILDING

1121 Capital Steet/1114 Texas Avenue

While Houston got its first telephone exchange in 1880 and a long-distance line to Galveston in 1883 through the Missouri and Kansas Telephone Company, Southwestern Bell Telephone Company consolidated and expanded service when it constructed its own Houston operations building in 1912. The seven-story Preston Main Office couldn't keep up with growth, and a two-story addition, known as the Fairfax Central Office, was constructed to the west in 1926. In 1938, two stories were added to the original building, and the addition gained six stories. The building has retained its original appearance and its interior has retained the original ground-floor elevator lobby, granite steps and chrome handrails.

Following World War II, Southwestern Bell expanding its Preston-Fairfax exchange again and moved into a new sixteen-story building. This Late Modern–style, buff-colored brick building, connected at the rear on multiple floors, sat between two other buildings, blocking any evidence of their connection. Southwestern Bell purchased the newer building in 1973 and modernized the complex in 1980. After consolidating into AT&T, the Texas Avenue property was sold, and the connections between the buildings were closed off. AT&T continues to own the Capitol Street Central Office building, and the other property was converted into a Hyatt hotel.

PETROLEUM BUILDING

1314 Texas Avenue

This twenty-two-story, stepped-back skyscraper was the first of its style in Houston and housed the offices of Joseph Cullinan's growing Texas Fuel Company, known today as Texaco. Constructed in 1926, the building is typical of other 1920s skyscrapers—a tall, thin tower rising slightly higher than the more solid-looking portion of the building. The painted name of later occupant Great Southwest Life vertically adorns the south wall in place of any windows. Reliefs on the upper floors were inspired by Mesoamerican design, and their stepped-back style is intended to mimic a Mayan pyramid.

The building's appearance has changed little over the years. While Texaco relocated to larger offices, the building served smaller oil and gas companies and Great Southwest Life. It was also home to the business oriented Tejas Club while retail operations rented space on the ground floor. More recently, the building has been renovated into a hotel.

KEYSTONE BUILDING

1120 Texas Ave

The Keystone Building, designed as a multi-tenant office building, opened in 1920. It is most well known as the home to famed Houston photographer Robert Bailey's Etchracft Studio from 1929 to 1934. The ten-story limestone and brick building features its name carved in a band between the entrance and the second-floor windows. Double entryway doors are flanked by black marble tile, which are flanked by lights fixed to the front façade. In 1975, the Keystone was converted into a document storage facility. During renovations, the company sealed all of the windows. Renovations came again in 1998, when the building was converted into the Keystone Lofts.

HOUSTON POST DISPATCH BUILDING

1100 Texas

This twenty-two-story Classical Revival–style building was the last one designed by Houston-based Sanguinet and Staats architecture firm. It was commissioned for Ross Sterling, a founder of Humble Oil Company, Houston National Bank and the city's first radio station (KPRC). Sterling also combined two struggling newspapers, the *Post* and *Dispatch*, which were housed here. This was set to be the largest, most expensive structure erected in Houston, and over eleven months in 1925 and 1926, Houstonians watched as the building went up in record time.

After Sterling was elected governor in 1930, the Great Depression hit, and he unloaded the newspaper and the building. Shell Oil moved in and remained until 1970. Modernizations followed—the interior was gutted, the main entrance portico was removed and much of the lower floor's ornamentation was destroyed. The building hosted various tenants through the mid-1990s before its conversion to the Magnolia Hotel.

HOUSTON BRANCH OF THE FEDERAL RESERVE BANK OF DALLAS

1301 Texas Street

Houston lost out to Dallas in 1914 when a site was chosen for the location of the Eleventh Federal Reserve District. Five years later, Houston applied for a branch bank, and the request was granted. This Neoclassical, three-story building opened in 1921. The building was in use as a bank until 1956, when the branch relocated. Over the next forty years, the building hosted a variety of companies before being purchased and renovated in 1998 as the new headquarters and central training facility for the Houston area Urban League. It has also served as home to the Harambee Art Gallery.

COTTON EXCHANGE BUILDING

1310 Prairie Avenue

Constructed in 1924, this building was the new home for the Cotton Exchange. This sixteen-story building cost $1.5 million to construct and featured a trading floor on the top story and a fifty-car garage in the basement that was accessed by a lift. Most of the offices of the members of the exchange were housed here, including the firm of Anderson, Clayton and Company, which relocated from Oklahoma City in 1916 and built a massive cotton operation along the new Houston Ship Channel.

As the principal tenant for a number of years, the company supervised twenty-four thousand employees worldwide from its eleventh-floor headquarters. It later diversified into textiles and food and was acquired by Quaker Oats Company. In 1993, the building underwent renovations and became the Anderson Clayton Courthouse Annex. The Anderson,

This photography features a slightly elevated view of the Houston and Texas Central railyards around 1904. The flatcars are loaded with bales of cotton—textiles and rail both being major industries in Houston and Texas. *Courtesy of Library of Congress.*

Clayton and Company founders placed an indelible footprint on Houston, creating the Texas Medical Center, the MD Anderson Cancer Center and numerous philanthropic endeavors.

DEGEORGE HOTEL

1418 Preston Street

Constructed of concrete and steel in 1913, the DeGeorge Hotel was one of Houston's first fireproof buildings. When the six-story hotel opened in January 1914, guests found a ground floor with large storefront windows, a spacious lobby that served as a convention hall, a west side café with a separate entrance and an east room allowing "drummers," or traveling salesmen, to display their goods. Eventually, the east side was filled with a tailor, barber, drugstore and pool room. The hotel was modern and elegantly furnished and offered telephones, hot and cold running water and a few rooms with their own private baths.

Michele DeGeorge, who came to Houston in 1884 and operated a grocery business, located his hotel near the new Union Station and along the electric streetcar line. His family continued to operate the hotel until 1978 when it was sold and renamed the King George Hotel. In 2000, the City of Houston renovated the building as the DeGeorge at Union Station and uses it as subsidized housing for low-income veterans.

WESTHEIMER BUILDING

1217 Prairie Street

This four-story building was constructed for Sidney Westheimer Company Undertakers in 1913, who called it home until the business moved into the Marine Building one block east in 1920. During the building's infancy, the fourth floor was known as Westheimer Hall and served as a meeting place for a handful of unions and associations.

The exterior and ground floor appearance has only changed slightly with reconfigured windows and the removal of the entryway's extension. Following the undertaker's residency, the building became the Foreman Building, and in the 1970s, the McFadden brothers moved their cotton exporting business into the building. Today, it is the Continental Center and houses a variety of office spaces.

CHRIST CHURCH CATHEDRAL

1117 Texas Avenue

Founded in 1839, Christ Church Cathedral was home to one of the city's first religious congregations, which continues worshipping on its original site. Following the advice of missionaries touting the new city as promising for evangelism, Colonel William Fairfax Gray moved his family from Virginia in 1839. He immediately began soliciting members and pledges for a building.

Construction could barely keep up with the congregation's growth. New buildings were constructed in 1845. A second building, which started in 1859, was slowed in part by the Civil War and wasn't finished until 1876. Expansion came again later that year and then again in 1893. The latter expansion included an ornate rood screen separating the chancel from the nave, memorial stained-glass windows, an 1880 altar cross and a new cloister. When the cloister was attached in 1938, a portion of the original structure collapsed, and a major fire nearly destroyed the chancel. In 1995, the church celebrated the fiftieth anniversary of its designation as the Cathedral of the Diocese of Texas.

UNION STATION

501 Crawford Street

By 1910, Houston had become Texas's primary railroad hub, and it had seventeen railways. In 1909, Houston Belt and Terminal Railway commissioned New York architects Warren and Wetmore to design a new railroad hub east of downtown. All structures in a twelve-block area were cleared, and construction began in December. Work went quickly. It began operating in August 1910, was dedicated the following March and two stories were added the following year.

Dedicated in 1911, the former hub of Houston's rail transportation now serves as a focal point in Minute Maid Park. Its construction called for the demolition of a major section of residential structures but added to the city's prominence as the main railroad hub of the southern United States. *Author's collection.*

Rising three stories, the Classical Revival station features a Crawford Street entrance, a portico supported by pillars and six decorative columns. Inside, three kinds of marble make up everything from lunchroom counters to waiting room wainscoting. First-floor waiting rooms were segregated, and the upper floors held railroad offices. Behind the main building stood umbrella sheds that covered a dozen tracks and a three-block freight depot.

Union Station remained the primary passenger terminal until 1974, when a considerably smaller Amtrak station opened in July. Used primarily for office space, the station was modernized, including the installment of ceiling panels, but it was restored to look similar to its original appearance in 2000 when it was incorporated into the design of Minute Maid Park, home to Major League Baseball's Houston Astros. In 2005, it was the site of the first World Series game to be played in Texas when the Astros faced the Chicago White Sox.

SAM HOUSTON HOTEL

1117 Prairie Street

Houston's Hotel Row, located along and near Prairie Street just blocks from Union Station, led directly into downtown. The 1924 Sam Houston Hotel set itself apart from its neighbors by catering to the city's newest visitor: traveling salesmen. These were budget-minded business travelers looking for a moderately priced room with the amenities of home.

At ten stories, plus a basement, this hotel featured street-fronted retail, including a coffee shop, a barber and beauty parlor, a haberdashery and a cigar/newsstand/drugstore, with two lobby entrances off Prairie and San Jacinto. The hotel closed its doors in 1975, and in 2000, preservation efforts brought the building closer to its original appearance. It reopened in 2002 as the Alden Hotel. It has since reverted to the original Sam Houston Hotel name and, along with the Tennison Hotel, is all that remains of Hotel Row.

ISIS THEATER

1008 Prairie Street

When it opened in 1912, the one-screen Isis Theater was one of Houston's first silent movie houses. It was situated diagonally across from the Rice Hotel, because Jesse Jones wanted to give guests something to do while staying in downtown Houston. The Isis continued as a theater until 1929, when the space was converted to house an expanding McCrory's five-and-dime store from the neighboring Wilson's Building. When McCrory's eventually closed, the buildings were separated.

A handful of tenants occupied the space over the years before it sat vacant during the 1990s. More recently, the space has housed a nightclub, dinner theater and brewery. Some remnants of the theater's original Egyptian décor from the interior are all that remain. The upper floors are now home to office space and the first floor and below is an underground beer garden and food hall.

MAFRIGE BUILDING

411 Fannin Street

The purpose of building on this land in 1905 was the construction of a warehouse for an expanding cotton exporting business. While designed to handle the heavy loading and equipment needed for storage of cotton, the warehouse's significant distance from rail and docks proved impractical. In 1908, Cargill Company, one of Houston's largest printing and engraving companies moved in instead. Cargill remained until 1936 when it was sold to the Mafrige family.

Extensive remodeling in 1950 changed the exterior appearance dramatically, covering the front façade with white granite, recessing the storefront and reconfiguring the windows. When the granite began to pull away in 1988, it revealed the destruction of much of the building's ornamentation. A new stucco finish was added, the original window configuration was restored and a new cornice was created to complete the upper façade. The name "Mafrige 1898–1998" was also added. The property still belongs to the Mafrige family, and several tenants lease space inside.

REPUBLIC BUILDING

1018–1022 Preston Street

The eight-story Republic Building, constructed in 1907, is one of the city's oldest skyscrapers, sitting on land originally intended to house the new county courthouse. Search the terra-cotta ornamentation for eagles and cartouches emblazoned with a *P* for Allen Paul, the developer. In 1910, the building served as home to the United States District Court, as well as the U.S. district attorney, U.S. marshal and jury rooms. Later tenants included the *Galveston-Dallas News*, the YMCA, Hoffman Oil Company, Turnbow Oil and Refining and future governor Ross Sterling's office. Renovations came in the 1950s, occupancy dwindled from 1970 until the early 1980s and today a variety of tenants, including a corner convenience store at street level, occupy the building.

HARRIS COUNTY COURTHOUSE

1001 Preston

The 1910 Harris County Courthouse occupies Courthouse Square, the site of Harris County government since 1837. Previous courthouses dating from 1838, 1851, 1860 and 1883 once stood here. The six-story Neoclassical courthouse is constructed of pink Texas granite and light brown pressed brick with terra-cotta, limestone and masonry ornamentation. A ring of eagles circles the central dome's base and inside is a five-story atrium that is capped by a stained-glass dome and a double-height courtroom with mezzanine.

A defeated bond issue in 1938 saved the courthouse from demolition, and while a new courthouse was built across San Jacinto in 1954, this building was remodeled for office space. Plans to reverse most of this restorative work arrived in 2003 and were completed in 2011. Today, it houses the first and fourteenth courts of appeals.

SCANLAN BUILDING

405 Main Street

Constructed atop the site of the Republic of Texas's President's House is the eleven-story Scanlan Building—the first in Houston to reach beyond the benchmark of ten stories. Kate Scanlan and her six sisters directed the commission of this building in 1909 as a monument to their father, Thomas Howe Scanlan, a three-term Houston mayor who died three years before.

Scanlan had purchased this land in 1865, hoping to build a large, modern office building, but he died before it could be realized. Because he was a widower, his estate passed to his unmarried daughters. The Scanlan has seen only slight alterations and currently houses office space.

Above: Occupying an entire city block, the Harris County Courthouse has served as the site of the seat of government in the county since 1837. It is the fifth courthouse to stand in this spot, set aside by the Allen brothers specifically for this purpose. *Author's collection.*

Left: The Scanlan Building, seen here in 1915, was built on the site of the first official home of the president of the Republic of Texas. It was the first in Houston to be built taller than ten stories. *Courtesy of Special Collections, University of Houston Libraries.*

FOLEY'S DEPARTMENT STORE

407 Main Street

Starting with a simple dry goods store in 1889, William L. Foley's business grew to be Houston's largest department store by 1922. After moving several times in the previous three decades, Foley opened a new location in this building. This operation was unique, as it sold only home furnishings. As it continued to grow, Foley's had a new building constructed a few blocks away in 1947.

San Antonio–based department store Joske's took over this building in October 1948, where it remained until the store closed the location in 1963. In 1987, Little Rock–based Dillard's purchased this building. In recent years, it has served primarily as the location for a variety of restaurants.

SWEENEY, COOMBS AND FREDERICKS BUILDING

301 Main Street

In March 1860, a major fire destroyed the south side of Main Street at Commerce. In its place, William Van Alstyne built a connected series of three-story Greek Revival brick buildings. In 1882, John Jasper Sweeney and Edward L. Coombs, purchased the corner section for their jewelry store and were joined by Gus Fredericks in 1889. That same year, another fire almost destroyed the building. This building rose from its ruins.

This narrow, three-story brick and stucco building features a rounded corner turret that rises above the roofline above the main entrance. The older "ruins" are evident in the inconsistent window spacing on the north side, due to an addition of seven feet of floor space. In 1891, the trio sold the building to Eugene Pillot but continued to operate their business for sixteen more years. Other tenants included Burgheim Drug Store, a cigar store and a men and boy's store before the Pillots sold the building to Harris County in 1941. Initially slated for demolition, Harris County instead restored and repurposed it for county offices and leased space, and it now houses a mixture of restaurant space and offices.

The Sweeney, Coombs and Frederick Building is one of the few Victorian buildings remaining in Houston. In 1882, the W.A. Van Alstyne Building sat here and was set to be demolished to make way for this newer building. There is speculation that the demolition was never completed but instead the building was incorporated by renovation into this building. *Author's collection.*

PILLOT BUILDING

1006 Congress/300 Fannin

The 1858 Pillot Building was one of the earliest iron-front buildings constructed west of the Mississippi River. The Greek Revival–style building serves as a landmark of Houston's progress with early tenants including attorneys, real estate brokers and a dry goods merchant. It later housed a hotel, a barbershop, restaurants and bars. The family of Eugene Pillot owned the building until 1944, and it was acquired by Harris County in 1975.

Sitting across from the Harris County Courthouse, the Pillot Building was prime real estate when the county purchased it in 1975. Though the plan was to replace it with a new administrative building, the county neglected the building until deterioration was so advanced that, in 1982, only three of the four exterior walls were still intact.

It was decided to restore the building, but during renovation work in 1988, the building collapsed. Despite this major setback, the project progressed, and a replica, incorporating some of the original cast iron columns, sills and lintels was completed in 1990. Today, the building is owned and operated by a law firm that offers meeting areas, conference rooms and event space inside.

WILLIAM L. FOLEY HOUSE

1617 Texas Avenue

William L. Foley, proprietor of the W.L. Foley Dry Goods Company, had this Victorian home built in 1904 in the tony Quality Hill neighborhood. Within months of its construction, the Houston Belt and Terminal Railway began buying up nearby properties for a new passenger station in a twelve-block area. Foley fought but ultimately sold his land in 1906, moving the home to 704 Chenevert in 1909.

When Foley died in 1923, the house remained in the family until 1963 when it was bequeathed to the Annunciation Catholic Church located across from the original home site. In 2003, the church sold the house to the City of Houston, which had it moved near its original location, next door to the Arthur B. Cohen house. After a regional tourism center project failed, the home was reclaimed by the church, which moved it back to its property for use as a parsonage.

ANNA STABE KERSTINGS BUILDING

417 San Jacinto Street

The Anna Stabe Kerstings Building has operated as a boardinghouse or hotel since its construction in 1904. Known today as the Londale Hotel, it is the city's longest-running hostelry building still on its original site.

Originally, the upper two stories were home to the boardinghouse operations while the ground floor featured a Houston Motor Car Company showroom.

ANNUNCIATION CATHOLIC CHURCH

1618 Texas Avenue

The 175-foot-tall Annunciation Catholic Church once served as a beacon inside the residential Quality Hill neighborhood. The congregation grew

Houston's Church of the Annunciation, next door to Minute Maid Park, remains the city's oldest existing church. It grew out of St. Vincent's, Houston's first Catholic church. *Author's collection.*

out of St. Vincent's, Houston's first Catholic church, and in 1866, plans for a Romanesque European–style cathedral began. Land was purchased, bricks were retrieved from the newly demolished Harris County Courthouse and construction began in 1869. In 1871, Annunciation was dedicated, and St. Vincent's closed just seven years later.

An enhanced bell tower came in 1871. The original tower was replaced with two smaller towers and the church added the clerestory level, higher ceilings, a transept, a fresco and a barreled and coffered ceiling. Later improvements included a sanctuary expansion in 1884 and the addition of marble alters, a rose window, a Pilcer pipe organ and technological advances moving into the middle of the century.

ARTHUR B. COHN HOUSE

1711 Rusk Avenue

This two-story, three-bedroom Queen Anne home located in Quality Hill started as another house altogether. Constructed in 1905 at the site of Winnifred Browne's 1860s home, the Arthur Benjamin Cohn House incorporated portions of its predecessor as flooring in the two-story kitchen wing.

The home changed hands in 1909, 1914 and 1935, before being converted into small apartments and eventually falling into disrepair. St. Francis Charities purchased the home in 1964. It's moved a few times since and has been restored. It is used as a training and distribution center for the charity's literature.

Located about a block away from its original location, this house was built for Arthur B. Cohn, personal accountant of William Marsh Rice. Elements of the house predate its construction, evidence that portions of the 1860s Winifred Browne home were incorporated or salvaged and reconstructed. *Author's collection.*

4

FOURTH WARD

COMMERCIAL NATIONAL BANK

116 Main Street

The 1904 Beaux-Arts Commercial National Bank building was the first skyscraper in what was once Houston's bustling financial district. The bank was chartered in 1886 with a capital of $500,000, making it one of the largest banks in the city. Following a 1912 merger with South Texas National Bank, it was replaced by the National Bank of Commerce, which was replaced by Western Union in 1915. Western Union was the building's primary tenant until 1970.

The upper floors were occupied by oil companies, the first offices of what is now Rice University, civil engineers and others. During the 1970s, the building was modernized but has since been reversed, with the ground-floor façade restored and the curved corner door reconstructed.

ABRAHAM WATKINS/HOGAN-ALLNOCH BUILDING

800 Commerce Street

Two separate structures, built at different times, make up this building located along Produce Row. The smaller Siewerssen Building was constructed in 1894 and served as a meat storage facility and market. The larger Dickson

Building was built in 1905 and was home to the Hogan-Allnoch Dry Goods Company. In 1971, the Hill, Kronzer and Abraham law firm, founded in 1951, purchased the vacant early Texas Federal–style building. Over the next few years, the firm restored the masonry, the heavily timbered second floor and the oak ceiling rafters. The firm moved into the renovated building in January 1975 and still occupies the space to this day.

B.A. REISNER BUILDING

900 Commerce Street

The Reisner Building, constructed in 1906, sat along Produce Row, but this three-story brick building is somewhat deceptive. Once housing a warehouse for Southern Rice Products Company, by the end of the twentieth century, the upper levels of the Reisner consisted only of historic façades facing Commerce and Travis Streets.

Located along Produce Row, the 1906 Reisner building sat in the heart of Houston's commercial district. The Houston chapter of the American Institute of Architects purchased this building to be the new home of Architecture Center Houston. In 2017, Hurricane Harvey dealt only a slight setback in opening. *Author's collection.*

The structure behind it had been removed for a parking lot, the upper-floor windows were infilled with brick and the doors and canopies were removed. Today, the brick façade and cornice details remain in good condition, and restoration of its original façade has brought it as close to the original as possible. It is now home to Houston's branch of the American Institute of Architects (AIA) and Architecture Center Houston (ArCH).

BAKER-MEYER BUILDING

313–15 Travis Street

Early Houstonian George Baker constructed this Greek Revival building around 1870. In 1884, Baker's daughter Rebecca married Joseph F. Meyer, whose family has owned the building since. It is the third-oldest commercial building in Houston. Joseph went on to found Joseph Meyer Hardware Company, serve as president of Houston National Exchange Bank and own more than six thousand acres in southwest Houston, a portion of which

Traveling north along the 300 block of Travis Street brings you to a couple of historic buildings that now house two Houston institutions. The Fox-Kuhlman Building (305–07 Travis) hosts the present (formerly relocated) location of Warren's Inn, and the Baker-Meyer Building (313–15 Travis) has been home to the Treebeards Restaurant since 1978. *Author's collection.*

would be developed as the Meyerland subdivision in 1955. In later years, this building housed tenants such as a feed store, a tailor shop, toy store and several nightclubs, and since 1978, it has been home to the Treebeards restaurant. During a 1990s renovation, a round brick and plaster cistern was discovered and is now gated and lighted for inspection. A mural depicting a market scene was completed in 1997, and a second-floor balcony was added in 1999.

BARRINGER-NORTON BUILDING

506 Main Street

Barringer-Norton moved its headquarters to this building in 1928. Originally constructed as a two-story brick building by Frederick Sawyer in 1878, it housed druggists, a cigar shop, a barber and other business over its early years. It received a Tudor Revival–style reconstruction of its façade in 1928 in an attempt to promote an air of high quality and style to the clothing line.

The clothing store moved to the Esperson Building in 1946. Zale's Jewelers moved into the vacant shop later that year and remodeled the first-floor storefront. Zale's left in 1962, and the building eventually lost its unique storefront façade. In the late 1990s, the first-floor façade was restored, and it now stands in contrast with its neighbors, just as it was intended to in 1928. Barringer-Norton became Norton Ditto, which survives as a company to this day.

BREWSTER BUILDING

108 Main Street

This mixed-use, three-story, slim, Italianate-style building constructed in 1873 was purchased by brothers-in-law John Anderson and Dave Edwards. It originally served early Houston businesses by housing offices and warehouse space and was home to the Houston Dry Goods and Notion warehouse. Composed of brick and stucco, the Brewster is one of the oldest commercial buildings in downtown Houston. Work over the years, most recently to get the building's image back to its original image, included a complete restoration of the existing façades and repairs to the original windows, masonry and plasterwork.

BYRD'S DEPARTMENT STORE

418–422 Main/919 Prairie

Designed in the Art Deco style, this building was designed specifically for use as a Byrd's Department Store, which opened in 1934. The three-story building features very little ornamentation and a corner entry at Prairie and Main Streets. The ground floor has large retail windows stretching down the street along the two primary façades with large, square inset windows on the upper two stories.

Over the years, several businesses have called the building home, including a market; a loan, jewelry and pawn shop; and, most recently, restaurants. In 2005, the Byrd Building underwent renovations to become Byrd's Lofts, using architect Joseph Finger's original blueprints as a guide but relocating its primary entrance from Main to Prairie Street.

CASINO SALOON

924 Congress Street

The domed, one-story brick building opened in 1882 and was a restaurant or saloon until Prohibition. The business originated as a seafood market and restaurant that also catered to people's homes. The original circle arch and barrel vault ceilings are still intact to this day, and a wall-to-wall skylight takes over the back half of the interior. Since that time, it has been home to a barber shop, the Circle Bar and the Red Cat Jazz Café. It is now home to OKRA (Organized Kollaboration on Restaurant Affairs) Charity Saloon. OKRA is a nonprofit group of bar and restaurant owners that advocate for small restaurant owners and give 100 percent of the bar's proceeds to local charities.

CITIZENS NATIONAL BANK

402 Main Street

James Bailey designed this 1925 Beaux-Arts building for Public National Bank at a time when Houston's Main Street was the city's epicenter of commerce. During the 1920s, Houston's financial district had begun to move southward along Main Street with several new bank buildings going up outside the older Victorian-era banking corridor. This nine-story building was one of Bailey's first major commissions. Over the years, it has served a multitude of tenants, most notably Citizens National Bank and Trust and later an art gallery and night club.

COTTON EXCHANGE BUILDING

202 Travis Street

This red-brick, low-rise Victorian Renaissance Revival building has been a fixture since 1884. During construction, architect Eugene Heiner added a personal touch—four angels carved into the façade, said to represent his four daughters. The building became a center for business and civic events. In addition to housing a saloon in the basement, it was home to a variety of offices, the exclusive Houston Club and the exchange room and galleries of the Houston Cotton of Change and Board of Trade. In 1907, an ornate trading room was added, and the building was enlarged by adding a fourth floor that was distinctly different from the façade below.

In 1924, the exchange moved to a new, sixteen-story building and took the original cornerstone of this building. It was not restored for use until 1973 and has since hosted a variety of businesses and restaurants. The Houston Cotton Exchange and Board of Trade continued for some time but disbanded in the 1970s.

DESEL-BOETTCHER WAREHOUSE

901–915 Commerce Street

The two-story Desel-Boettcher Produce Company warehouse opened in 1903 on Commerce Street, which was known as Produce Row. Formed by Charles M. Desel and Frederick A. Boettcher, it was one of the largest produce companies in the Southwest, purchasing goods from vegetable commission companies and selling it to retail grocers. A large sign painted on the warehouse greeted boats coming to the bayou's Main Street landing.

Desel-Boettcher thrived as a major source of produce in Houston for years. The building was later used by a pharmaceutical company and as

The 1884 incarnation of the Houston Cotton Exchange added a fourth floor in 1907 and continued to use the building until a replacement was built in 1924. It has since been restored and earned Preservation Houston's Good Brick Award in 1979. *Author's collection.*

Severely flooded and damaged during Hurricane Harvey in 2017, longtime resident Spaghetti Warehouse shut down, sold off much of its interior decorations and relocated under a redesigned banner in 2019. The building continues to undergo restoration and reimagining but remains a focus on the local haunted scene. *Author's collection.*

a Southern Pacific Railroad storehouse. From 1974 to 2017, the Spaghetti Warehouse called the building home, decorating it with items from Houston's past, including seating inside an old trolley. In 2017, the building suffered greatly from Hurricane Harvey, forcing the Spaghetti Warehouse to find new digs. The warehouse awaits a new tenant and is now occupied only by the ghosts of its past occupants.

DIXON BUILDING

110 Milam Street

The four-story, brick Dixon building was constructed in 1890 and once served as part of the Magnolia Brewing Company complex. During Prohibition, the brewery's buildings were put to other uses. Alterations to the building came in 1925, for reuse by the Dixon Packing Company. The building was severely damaged by floods in 1929 and 1935, and these eventually undermined or destroyed significant portions of the building.

The Magnolia Brewery never recovered after Prohibition, and with the flood damage, the company closed for good in 1950. This cold storage building was abandoned and quickly became a vacant and broken shell. For nearly three decades, it sat empty until it was redeveloped as a nightclub topped with residential lofts on the upper floors. Since then, it has housed restaurants, a flea market, Stages Theater and the Blaffer Art Museum. The ragged edges remain, now with glass shaped to fit the gaps in the wall left by the 1935 flooding. Nothing remains of the ice factory or the main brewery on the north side of the bayou.

DORRANCE BUILDING

114 Main Street

This Italian Renaissance building is named after John W. Dorrance, founder of Dorrance & Co., one of Houston's oldest cotton firms. Constructed out of gray bricks furnished by the St. Louis firm of Hydraulic Press Brick Company, the building became home to the Postal Telegraph Company and a handful of banking companies, including Jesse Jones's National Bank of Commerce. Other tenants of this 1903 structure included the law offices of Baker and Botts, the Southern Pacific Railroad Company and the office of William Marsh Rice, which, following his death in 1900, became the first offices of Rice Institute (now Rice University). In 1915, Western Union moved in and took over the building, remaining its principal tenant until 1970. Western Union oversaw a massive renovation of the building in 1931, when a fifth floor was added.

FOX-KUHLMAN BUILDING

305–07 Travis Street

The two-story, brick Fox-Kuhlman Building fronts two separately owned and occupied halves of one building. Located on the site of John and Eliza Fox's bakery that burned in 1860, the Fox-Kuhlman Building was constructed from 1862 until 1866 and was sold to Henry Stude in the 1860s. His children and grandchildren would continue the business, which became a prominent commercial bakery lasting into the mid-twentieth century.

Despite the continuous façade, each half of the Fox-Kuhlman Building has the appearance of two separate façades. At 307 Travis, the south half, the original façade prevails, featuring double front doors flanked by narrower doors, transom lights and brick window hoods. This portion has seen a succession of restaurants and bars with Warren's Inn residing there since the 1980s. The north half, at 305 Travis, has seen more extensive alterations, with some exterior work in 2001 to garner a more authentic, historic look. It would later house Duke of Hollywood, a tailor still in operation today.

GEORGE HERMANN ESTATE BUILDING

204 Travis Street

Standing at seven stories, this 1917 structure was commissioned by the estate of George Henry Hermann. Hermann accumulated a personal fortune through various business enterprises and donated much of the land on which Hermann Park now sits. He also funded what is now known as

Looking north along the 200 block of Travis, you'll stretch toward the Bayou (but not quite make it). Along the way, you'll pass William Foley's Dry Goods Store (214–218 Travis), the George Hermann Estate Building (204 Travis) and the 1884 Cotton Exchange and Board of Trade (202 Travis). *Author's collection.*

Memorial Hermann Hospital. The Neoclassical building was designed to house cotton industry personnel and was later used as the headquarters, or Area Command, for the Salvation Army of the Greater Houston Area. In 1996, it was sold, renovated and converted into the Hermann Lofts.

HENRY BRASHEAR BUILDING

910 Prairie Street

In 1882, Henry Brashear had this three-story Victorian building constructed right in the heart of the city's thriving commercial district. Brashear was born in the Republic of Texas and served as criminal district court clerk for Harris County. Over the years, the Brashear building has housed a variety of tenants, starting with druggist Erwin Erlenmeyer. Later inhabitants included jewelers Gorman and McAughan (who stayed for forty-five years), a children's clothing store, dry cleaners and a dry goods store. The building also included storage space, some furnished rented rooms on the upper floors and, more recently, restaurants. It was fully restored in the 1990s and continues to include, in the rear of the building, what may be Houston's oldest water closet.

HENRY HENKE BUILDING

801–05 Congress Street

Serving as the location of a Henke's grocery store, this three-story building was constructed in 1928, with renovations in 1948. Today, it contains a fourth floor. Throughout the twentieth century, Henke & Pillot was one of the largest grocery operations in the city, and by 1956, it had twenty-seven stores throughout southeast Texas. Purchased in the 1950s by Cincinnati-based Kroger Company, when it expanded operations into Houston, it began phasing out the Henke & Pillot name. Out front, "Henke & Pillot" is embedded in tiles stretching twenty feet along the sidewalk between storefront and street. In 1981, the owners of the building received Preservation Houston's Good Brick Award for their restoration work.

Henry Henke, who operated a grocery from this and several other locations, began his supermarket enterprise in 1872. Henke visited Houston from New Orleans in 1872 to establish his new company, brought on Camille Pillot to become his bookkeeper in 1882 and made him a full partner a few years later. In 1955, Kroger acquired the chain and, in 1966, phased out the Henke and Pillot name. *Author's collection.*

HOGG BUILDING

401 Louisiana Street

The eight-story Art Deco Hogg Building was designed to be the Armor Building but opened as the Great Southern Building in March 1921. Inspired by the work of Louis Sullivan, the design called for concrete with reinforced steel, eliminating the need for a large number of piers. It housed Great Southern Life Insurance offices, along with a variety of other companies, including Armor Auto Company's ground-floor showroom.

William Clifford Hogg, eldest son of Texas governor Jim Hogg, used the eighth-floor, eighteen-room Spanish Revival–style penthouse (almost completely hidden from view when standing at street level) to manage Hogg Brothers Company and the families' philanthropic projects. In the 1920s, this elegant workspace was surrounded by a roof garden filled with shrubs and flowers and filled with the works of Frederic Remington. The family continued to use the penthouse as a business office until 1941. In the early 1990s, the building was converted into the Hogg Palace Lofts, opening in the fall of 1995.

HOUSTON NATIONAL BANK

202 Main Street

Houston National Bank, founded in 1876 as Fox Bank, moved into this new building in 1928. Humble Oil founder Ross S. Sterling had purchased the bank in 1926 and commissioned his son-in-law's firm, Hedrick and Gottleib to design the new headquarters. The three-story limestone and granite building features cast-bronze doors and thirty-five-foot columns facing each street. Inside is a five-story rotunda, a bronze fresco and a vaulted ceiling finished with mosaic tile, then second in height only to one New York bank.

The Islamic Houston Da'Wah Center is home to downtown Houston's first mosque and first location dedicated to Da'Wah, focusing on promoting Islamic principles, history and culture. The restored Houston National Bank, acquired by former Houston Rocket Hakeem Olajuwon in 1994, features a prayer hall, a gathering area, meeting rooms, classrooms, a guest suite, administrative offices, a kitchen, a library and a recreational facility. *Author's collection.*

It was the last of the new banks to be built on Main Street. Houston National Bank moved out in 1964 and was replaced by the Downtown Bank, which became Franklin Bank and left in 1975. Plans to turn the building into an Islamic center began in 1994, and in 2002, Houston's first downtown mosque opened, committed for Da'wah.

KENNEDY BAKERY

813 Congress Street

The Kennedy Bakery Building is likely the oldest Houston building that exists on its original site. Baker John Kennedy came to Texas via Ireland, New Jersey and Missouri in 1842. That fall, he opened his first bakery and then this building in 1860. It served a variety of proprietors before becoming William Berry's La Carafe in 1970. *Max Smith.*

The oldest commercial building in Houston, constructed in 1847, is a bar. This narrow, two-story, brick structure housing La Carafe is covered in nostalgic ephemera—old paintings, photos, newspaper clippings, sheet music and taxidermy fill the walls. Tall bare windows front the building, and a chandelier and candlesticks emit just enough light to conduct business. Outside, the exposed brick, concrete and wood on the right side showcases the building's remodeling. A small, wooden and very narrow staircase in the back leads upstairs.

Constructed in 1847 by Nathaniel Kellum, the building housed a variety of business throughout its existence, a trading post, stage stop, slave market, coffeehouse, drugstore and hair salon. Aside from its current use, it was best known as John Kennedy's bakery. During the Civil War, Kennedy obtained a contract to produce hardtack (a cracker-like baked good) for the Confederate army and leased other property to the Ordnance Office.

The building became a bar in the mid-1950s, and La Carafe arrived just a few years later. Be mindful, the bar only takes cash and uses a 1907 cash register to ring up sales.

KIAM BUILDING

320 Main Street

Built specifically for Edward Kiam's haberdashery in 1893, this building featured retail operations on the ground floor and office space above. The five-story, red-brick building is highlighted by its deeply recessed bullnose, corner-bay display window and featured one of the first electric passenger elevators in Houston.

Another retailer, the department store chain Sakowitz's, operated in the building from 1918 to 1929 before relocating to the Gulf Building. The exterior of the building faced very little alterations over the years, but the interior was modified numerous times to manage the needs of tenants before undergoing extensive restoration in 1981.

Looking south down the 300 block of Main Street. This historic stretch runs along Houston's light rail system. Stretching from the corner, you'll find the Sterne Building (300 Main), Stuart Building (304 Main), Sweeney and Coombs Building (310 Main) and the distinctly marked Kiam Building (320 Main), among others in the distance. *Author's collection.*

MAGNOLIA BREWERY BUILDING

715 Franklin Street

Hugh Hamilton came to Houston by way of Scotland, Philadelphia and San Antonio in 1893. He founded the Houston Ice and Brewing Company, a successful ice plant that was overshadowed by what would become the largest brewery in Houston, covering forty acres of downtown along the Buffalo Bayou. Expanding to both sides of the bayou over the next decade, the brewery's complex consisted of ten buildings by 1915. It was recognized as one of the best breweries in the nation.

When the brewery expanded across the bayou to Franklin Street in 1912, Hamilton had this two-story Italianate building constructed. It sits partially over the bayou and is connected to buildings on the north bank by a concrete platform. It served as the company's executive offices, a taproom and the home to the Magnolia Café.

This remainder of the Magnolia Brewing Company was used as the company's executive offices and taproom. It was built in 1912 and now serves as a rental ballroom. By 1915, Houston Ice and Brewing Company had grown to ten buildings and covered more than twenty acres on both sides of Buffalo Bayou. Prohibition chipped away at the brewery's prominence while a historic 1935 flood finally dragged it under. The brewery closed in 1950. *Author's collection.*

Magnolia Brewery adjusted its business to survive Prohibition but was not as lucky against Mother Nature. A major flood in 1935 caused extensive damage to the complex from which the brewery never fully recovered. It ultimately closed its doors in 1950. The Magnolia Building, now restored and renovated, operates as a special event venue, and remnants of an old transport bridge under the Louisiana Street Bridge are all that remain of the brewery's extensive network of buildings.

MARKET SQUARE PARK

Travis, Milam, Congress and Preston Streets

Entered into the National Register of Historic Places as part of the Main Street Market Square Historic District, Market Square Park has been a geographic and civic centerpiece since the city's founding in 1836. The land was donated to the city by Augustus Allen in 1854, and it was used as an open-air produce market. Early landmarks bordering the park were the Republic of Texas Capitol, the Republic's White House, four city hall buildings and the now demolished Market Square Building, which previously housed the city market. The park, established in 1976, is the centerpiece of the historic district and is Houston's largest and most intact group of civic and commercial history, representing architecture dating from 1858 and containing fifty-two buildings, the Main Street Viaduct and Allen's Landing Park.

MOSK BUILDING

508–10 Main Street

Constructed in the 1880s, this building features load-bearing brick sidewalls that are sixteen inches thick and supported by a series of cast-iron round columns that run the east–west axis of the building. Around 1920, the existing Victorian era façade was altered, and this two-story buff brick building became home to Victory Wilson, a Dallas-based clothing store. The retail operation had a short life in Houston, going out of business in the mid-1930s. A variety of companies moved in and out over the years, including Golden Stein, Esther Imports and Mosk's Store for Men. It was restored in 2009.

PEDEN IRON AND STEEL

110–12 Travis Street

This building, erected in 1890, stands as one of the original three buildings constructed for Peden Iron and Steel Company in Houston. This two-story brick building is clad in plaster and painted white. Peden Iron and Steel Company remained at this location until about 1906. It needed to expand and constructed its first building, which still stands, at 600 North San Jacinto. This Travis Street building remained to serve the Davidson Brothers business for wholesale cigars and tobacco. Later tenants included Schopmeyer Hardware, Lang and Frucht Wholesale Produce, Kincaide-Richards Fountain Supplies, Houston Fruit Auction Company and Jamail Produce Company.

RAPHAEL BUILDING

110 Main Street

Constructed in 1876, the three-story Raphael Building sits wedged between two other historic Houston structures. The façade of the three-story Italianate brick building originally matched that of the neighboring Brewster Building at 108 Main Street. During the most recent restoration work in 2016, the building's original interior brick walls were uncovered, hidden under nearly three inches of layered plaster and wallpaper that built up over years of remodeling. The owners, while converting the space into a bar, attempted to match the interior to the structure's original identity, including the removal of a modern tiled ceiling for a tin one and the removal of a fire escape that climbed the Main Street façade from street level to the roof.

RICE HOTEL

909 Texas Avenue

This was the site of the Republic of Texas Capitol before it moved to Austin, and the building was razed in 1857. In its place Capitol Hotel was built. It was later renamed the Rice after civic leader William Marsh Rice. Jesse Jones

This is the third Rice Hotel, seen here in 1916, to stand on this location. It sits on the site of the former capitol of the Republic of Texas. The capitol operated as a hotel until it was torn down in 1881. It was renovated and turned into apartments in 1998 after sitting vacant for twenty-one years. *Courtesy of Special Collections, University of Houston Libraries.*

purchased and leveled that hotel in 1911, replacing it with this seventeen-story building that opened in 1913.

The C-shaped hotel featured four restaurants, a small concert hall and a rooftop deck. A third wing was added in 1925, the rooftop was converted into the Petroleum Club of Houston in 1951 and a five-story "motor lobby" was installed in 1958. The Rice featured some of the first air-conditioned spaces in the city, was one of the first to use fluorescent lighting and was the first with an escalator.

Additionally, the Rice hosted a 1962 meeting of NASA astronauts—each checking in as "Max Peck"—where they discussed the future of space travel. President Kennedy and the first lady spoke here to the LULAC convention on the night of November 21, 1963. Other notable guests included Franklin Roosevelt during the 1928 Democratic National Convention, Texas governor William Hobby, Groucho Marx, Liberace and many others.

From 1956 to 1971, Houston Endowment operated the hotel before passing it on to the landowner, Rice University. Proving too costly to operate, and after several ownership changes, the hotel was left vacant. In 1987, a developer renovated the hotel into lofts, modeling the design after the 1913 Rice Hotel, including the two-story lobby, the Crystal Ballroom and the Empire Room, while reserving twenty-five thousand square feet of retail space on the ground floor. In 1998, the Post Rice Lofts, now known solely as the Rice Lofts, reopened.

RITZ THEATER

911 Preston Avenue

When the Ritz was built in 1926, there were twenty-five theaters in or near a six block stretch of Main Street. This is the only one that remains. The movie house could seat more than one thousand people and was designed in a colorful Renaissance style by William Ward Watkin, head of Rice Institute's department of architecture.

Local entrepreneur Will Horowitz took over operations in an alliance formed with the Interstate Theater chain in 1930. Renamed the Teatro Ritz (and later Cine Ritz) during the early 1940s, the theater began running Spanish-language films. In the 1970s, it was acquired by Alvin Guggenheim, who featured exploitation films and renamed it the Majestic Metro. The theater closed briefly for restoration work, including the installation of the iconic Majestic Metro sign. It reopened in 1990 as an event venue.

SCHOLIBO BUILDING

912 Prairie Avenue

When the need for a new building arose for Charles and Mary Scholibo to house their confectionary and bakery business, they decided on the design of this building. This 1880 Italianate commercial building was originally only sixty feet deep and finished off with a rear courtyard. The first floor was extended in 1882 and the second floor in 1913. During the 1950s, the exterior was extensively renovated, and the arched doorways were removed for the installation of a single recessed entrance flanked by a large window display.

A physician/surgeon, an auto livery and several laundries, drugstores and theaters all called the Scholibo home, but the Shoe Market was synonymous with the building from 1918 until 1971. In 1996, new owners began restoration work and returned it to much of its original design by 1999— even using salvaged wood shelving from the Shoe Market.

SOUTHERN PACIFIC RAILROAD BUILDING

915 Franklin Street

After acquiring the Houston to New Orleans route of the Texas and New Orleans Railway and the Houston to San Antonio route of the Buffalo Bayou, Brazos and Colorado Railway, the Southern Pacific Railroad located its regional offices in Houston. Serving as headquarters for eighty-five years, this 1910 building was designed by famed Chicago architect Jarvis Hunt and helped play a role in attracting the oil industry to Houston.

Designed to showcase a southwestern Native American pattern, the brick building includes abstract ornamentation and a façade scored with a red mortar pattern around blue tile. The building was sold in the late 1990s, following the merger of Denver-based Southern Pacific Railroad Corporation with Nebraska-based Union Pacific Railroad Corporation and has since been renovated and converted into the Bayou Lofts.

STATE NATIONAL BANK BUILDING

412 Main Street

The 1923 Spanish Colonial–style State National Bank Building rises fourteen floors and is one of the few surviving early Neoclassical skyscrapers in Texas. Established in 1915 as the State Bank and Trust Company, it continued to operate under that name until 1946, when it merged with First National Bank and moved out.

The skinny brick building is capped with one of the most unique Houston rooftops: an octagonal, red-tiled penthouse topped with a bronze lantern that is setback and nearly impossible to see except from a distance. The exterior features abound and include Greek heroes, ornamentations, engravings and an elaborate frieze at the entrance. It has an enormous marble-clad main lobby. Following the exit of the bank, the exterior façade and much of the interior was removed or altered. However, in 1982, renovations brought the building back to much of its original appearance and character.

STEGEMAN BUILDING

502–04 Main Street

Few remnants of Houston's Victorian era remain standing, but one that does still exist is the Stegeman Building. This two-story corner building was constructed by Frederick W. Stegeman in 1879 to house his ornamental ironwork business. It has seen its fair share of alterations with the removal of its mansard roof and window detailing. A third floor was added in 1890 but has since been removed.

A slipcover was added in the 1970s, but it did not fully obscure the upper ornamental brackets and the building's cornice, allowing future owners to discover the original design. They removed the slipcover and began restoration work to the original, hidden façade. Tenants of the building have included Church's Chicken, the offices of Houston East and West Texas Railway, Pullman Palace Car Company, an adult movie theater, dry goods vendors, a variety of medical offices, photography studios, a cigar store and several saloons, restaurants and bars.

STERNE BUILDING

300 Main Street

Buildings being destroyed by fire in nineteenth-century Houston were not entirely uncommon occurrences. The buildings located along this stretch of Main Street grew out of the ashes of their predecessors but stand strong in their stead.

The Sterne Building was built in 1916 by Pauline Sterne Wolff to replace her father's 1884 building that went up in flames. Matching the size, but not the appearance, of Sam Sterne's original building, occupants included the clothing and shoe store Krupp and Tuffly and Cockrell's Drug Store on the ground level, with the fraternal organization Thalian Club above.

STUART BUILDING

304 Main Street

The Stuart Building at 304 Main went up in 1880, following a massive fire in July 1879 that destroyed half of the block and is one of downtown's few remaining Victorian buildings. It was built at the same time and by the same owner as its neighbors to the south, 306 and 308 Main Street. Appearing as three separate buildings, the row shows a continuous construction line in the rear.

It housed a variety of attorneys and dentists on the upper floors, and ground floor tenants have included booksellers and jewelry stores. While much of the first-floor façade and design elements were removed or deteriorated by the 1920s, the Stuart Building still features many original Italianate features.

SWEENEY AND COOMBS BUILDING

310 Main Street

Prior to purchasing the Van Alstyne Building to house its jewelry business, Sweeney and Coombs jewelry store occupied a three-story Victorian masonry building, which was considered one of the most ornate buildings in Houston at the time. Built in 1880, it features an Italianate façade and a large clock between the second and third story. This was installed because the building and its neighbors ended up blocking the view of the city hall clock in Market Square.

Sweeney and Coombs grew out of Sweeney's pawn brokerage and exists today as Sweeney and Company Jewelry. Grunewald's Music Store occupied the building through much of the late 1800s, while the YWCA, the Musician's Protective Association Local no. 55, Hill-O-Music and Day Clothiers all operated out of the building over the years before AC Bowers took over ownership.

During the 1950s and 1960s, Day Clothiers remodeled the entire building, covering the ornate exterior plaster with a concrete slab on the upper floors and destroying an elaborate cornice and the original iron storefront and causing severe structural damage by installing an elevator. In the 1990s, following fifteen years of vacancy and standing partially roofless, a new owner began renovations. During the process they removed ten thirty-cubic-yard dumpsters of debris. They also removed the black façade, resculptured the original stucco and rebuilt the cornice and iron storefront.

UNION NATIONAL BANK

220 Main Street

The twelve-story Beaux-Arts Union National Bank Building opened in 1912 as one of the nation's first concrete and steel skyscrapers. Housed in a façade of stone and brick and trimmed with terra-cotta and stone, the Union National Bank was independent of all utilities, boasting its own heating, electric light plant and chilled-air system. Its design features keystones carved as Mercury (the Roman god of commerce and trickery), Corinthian columns outside and Doric columns inside, reaching up into an ornate, coffered ceiling.

In later years, the building became known as the Continental Building, the Pan Am Building and the Natural Gas Building, but by 1973, only five tenants remained above the second floor. In 2004, the building was transformed for the Hotel ICON, a boutique hotel. It has retained its outside exterior, but the interior now has a more contemporary look.

Now the Hotel Icon, this Beaux-Arts building features keystones carved as Mercury, the Roman god of commerce. The building was the first to tie Jesse Jones with Gulf Oil founder and Union National investor Andrew Mellon. *Author's collection.*

WILLIAM L. FOLEY DRY GOODS BUILDING

214–18 Travis Street

When John Kennedy died in 1878, his son-in-law William Foley moved his dry goods business into his 1860 building. Foley operated in the space for a decade before a fire nearly destroyed the two northernmost sections of the building. He had a new building constructed next door and remodeled the face of the remaining original.

The brick, stucco and stone-trimmed, three-story Renaissance Revival building features a sidewalk canopy with cast-iron columns that covers the entry. Following another fire in 1888, a third bay was added for Foley's expanding business. In the mid-1950s, the building underwent renovations. The first-floor entry was recessed, and plate glass windows were installed. Wood panels were installed below the windows in the 1970s.

Foley's was a chain of department stores started and based out of downtown Houston. Founded as Foley Brothers in 1900, the chain expanded to Texas, Colorado, Louisiana, Arizona, Oklahoma and New Mexico. In 2006, Foley's store names were phased out and rebranded as Macy's. *Courtesy of Special Collections, University of Houston Libraries.*

Foley's continued operating until 1948, and when Foley's daughter, Blanche, died in 1963, she left this property to the Sisters of the Incarnate Word. Following a fourth fire in 1989 (the third was in 1979), the building sat vacant but was purchased in the mid-1990s and was renovated from the inside out, reopening as a first-floor art gallery space with two apartments on the second floor. In 2008, the building was preserved in its original style and a restaurant began operation.

ANTIOCH MISSIONARY BAPTIST CHURCH

313 Robin Street

In January 1866, a small group of freed slaves organized Houston's first African American Baptist church. Members met at various locations before coming together under a bush arbor that was erected on the edge of Buffalo Bayou. As membership grew, a box house structure was constructed on Baptist Hill. The congregation swelled under Reverend Jack Yates, and in 1873, land was purchased for a new church, which opened in 1879.

Located in the heart of Freedmen's Town, it was the first brick structure built and owned by African Americans in Houston. Members played a major role in Houston's history, helping to establish the city's first African American public library; the city's first hospital for black patients and physicians, Union Hospital; and the precursor of Texas Southern University. They also worked with the NAACP to abolish Texas's notorious "white primary" law.

Over the years the building was enlarged and enhanced, including the addition of a second floor, a wing on the south and west, a baptistery, a pipe organ, ceiling fans and in 2003, the now-iconic "Jesus Saves" neon sign. Additionally, the church is known for its pointed arch windows and doors, and members worship on the original handmade pews.

BANK OF THE SOUTHWEST

910 Travis Street

Originally home to the Bank of the Southwest, this twenty-four-story building was constructed from 1953 to 1956. It was the first in Houston with a shell composed of an all-aluminum curtain wall. The Florence Knoll–designed lobby featured the commissioned thirteen-by-forty-five-foot mural *America* by Rufino Tamayo.

It was the first of the original three buildings in downtown to be networked into the city's tunnel system, connecting it to the Commerce Building and the Ten-Ten Garage. The building underwent a massive modernization renovation in the early 1990s—the mural was sold to a private collector in 1993 and a three-hundred-space parking garage was installed. Additional renovations were completed in early 2007. The building has also been home to Bank One, PM Realty, the United States District Attorney's office and the offices for the U.S. District Court for the Southern District of Texas.

BATTELSTEIN'S DEPARTMENT STORE BUILDING

812 Main Street

When Battelstein's opened this ten-story building in 1950, the front featured a deeply recessed entry with large picture windows lining the ground floor, but the rest of it was utilitarian, featuring little to no ornamentation. Retail wars forced Battelstein's to keep up with competitors, so it enlarged and remodeled the store along the way. The company, founded by Battelstein brothers Abe, Harry and Bennie, was purchased by Beall's in the early 1970s, and it has since merged with Palais Royal. It closed the downtown location in 1980, and the building sat abandoned for nearly thirty years. Its storefront received a mural painting before being purchased in 2018 by neighboring JW Marriott.

CARTER BUILDING

806 Main Street

When finished in 1910, the Carter Building was the first steel-framed skyscraper in Houston, and at sixteen-stories, it remained the city's tallest building from 1911 until 1926. Samuel Fain Carter, founder of Lumberman's National Bank, commissioned Sanguinet and Staats to design what would be derided as Carter's folly—too tall to be sound and too far away from the business core.

The air-conditioned building featured a basement bank vault, a Classical banking hall and an elaborate roof garden (later known as the Top o' Houston). Additions came in 1919, 1923 and 1955, making the building larger and more elaborate with additional stories, a penthouse and an elaborate board room. First National Life Insurance purchased and remodeled the building in the late 1960s with a redesigned lobby and glass and marble slipcover. In 2009, the Carter Building was sold. Restoration work removed all damaged ornamentation and the slipcover and remodeled the interior. The JW Marriot Houston Downtown opened in late 2014.

THE ESPERSON BUILDINGS

808 Travis Street (Niels)

815 Walker Street (Mellie)

The Niels and Mellie Esperson Buildings stand as monuments to a Houston couple's love. Mellie Esperson built the first of these two buildings in 1927 as a monument to her husband, Niels, an early investor in the Humble oil field who died in 1922. The nineteen-story Mellie Esperson Building was constructed in 1939 as an annex, allowing the two to remain side by side.

The thirty-two-story Niels skyscraper is the only complete example of the Italian Renaissance style in downtown Houston and was the third-tallest building in America when completed. It features a gold-leaf tower topped by an elaborate six-story tiered monument, mimicking one in Rome's San Pietro courtyard. Carved above the entrance is Niels's name. The inside features terra-cotta urns, bronze elevator doors, arabesque obelisks and imported Roman marble. The attached Mellie annex was Houston's largest office space. Her name is also carved in the building's façade, and both are illuminated at night.

Mellie thrived as a local businesswoman and real estate developer until her death in 1945. She managed her business and supported several organizations from her twenty-fifth-story offices. In the 1980s, the Esperson Buildings were connected to the tunnel system below Houston and, in the early 2000s, underwent a major redesign of the lobby and tunnel space.

The *tempietto* peeking out atop the Niels Esperson Building. Designed by theater architect John Eberson, it is the only complete example of Italian Renaissance architecture in downtown Houston. *Author's collection.*

93

FARM CREDIT BUREAU

430 Lamar Street

This three-story building with limestone façade opened in 1929. The Spanish Colonial Revival bank originally provided long-term, low-interest loans to area farmers and ranchers. The bank is the product of a 1988 merger between the Federal Land Bank of Texas and Federal Intermediate Credit Bank of Texas, which were both based in Houston since their respective founding in 1916 and 1923, before relocating to Austin in 1982.

Today, the Farm Credit Bank Building sits in the shadow of the neighboring glass Chevron Texaco Heritage Building, to which it is now attached, and is the second component of Heritage. This fifty-three-story skyscraper complex was developed in the 1980s and included the purchase of the bank building, which was renovated in 1978. As it was in excellent condition, the decision was made to incorporate the building itself and to mirror some of its design elements. The complex's larger tower is unique along the Houston skyline, featuring a Mayan rooftop design.

FIRST UNITED METHODIST CHURCH

1320 Main Street

Houston's Methodist church began shortly after the city's founding when missionaries established a Sunday School Society. Its first building opened in 1844 but sustained heavy damage during an 1860 storm, forcing the congregation to seek a new location. In 1883, the members returned to a newly constructed Charles Shearn Memorial Methodist Episcopal Church South at 801 Texas Avenue. This remained until 1907, when downtown development drove a desire for a new location.

The church sold the building, began meeting in Alabambra Hall and Beach's Auditorium and purchased land for development. In 1910, the new First Methodist Episcopal Church South, opened its doors. The Gothic-style church features a long porched entrance along Main Street, a four-story spire and large pointed-arch windows. In 1929, the congregation added a new education center next door.

A name change came in 1939 and again in 1968, becoming First United Methodist Church. Churchgoers are welcomed to a large sanctuary with

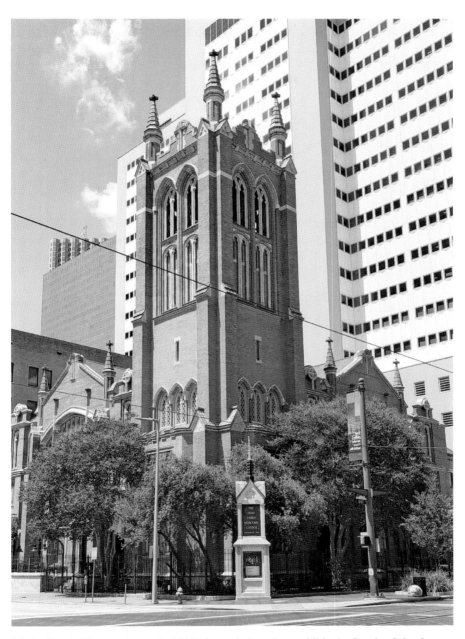

Methodism in Houston began in 1837 when missionaries established a Sunday School Society. In 1844, the Methodist Episcopal Church South opened its first building. The church grew, moved and has expanded to a second campus. *Author's collection.*

ornate stained-glass windows and an Aeolian-Skinner pipe organ that features more than seven thousand pipes. The church began offering televised worship services starting in 1955 and opened its Westchase campus in 1983.

GULF BUILDING

710–24 Main Street

The three-building Gulf Oil complex started as a thirty-six-story building. From its completion in 1929 until 1931, the Gulf Building was the tallest building west of the Mississippi River, and it dominated the skyline until 1963. It's first tenants included Gulf Oil, National Bank of Commerce and Sakowitz Brothers Department Store.

This Art Deco skyscraper originally housed an observation deck with two searchlight beacons and a telescope that topped the building. Three entrances lead to a two-story lobby that is decorated with eight frescoes featuring an illustrated history of Texas and Houston.

Thirteen- and sixteen-story annexes were added in 1946 and 1949. A large stained-glass window depicting the Battle of San Jacinto was installed in 1960. The observation deck's features were removed, and a fifty-three-foot rotating Gulf Oil sign was installed in the early 1960s—lasting until 1974. Additional modernization included covering windows, removing counters and a staircase and installing carpet. In the early 1980s, the building underwent one of the largest privately funded preservation projects by new the owner, Texas Commerce Bank. Additional restoration work followed in 2004.

HERMANN SQUARE

901 Bagby Street

The small Hermann Square sits at the foot of city hall and is dominated by a reflecting pool. This land was the homestead where George Hermann was born in 1843. Upon his death in 1914, the land for the square was given to the city. Houston made improvements, giving it a cross-axial plan and placing a centralized fountain in 1929. Grander plans that were canceled by the onset of the Great Depression called for lengthening the square and adding an orthogonal pool and alleys of live oak trees.

This simple park is used regularly for festivals, gatherings and concerts. An elevated plaza leads into city hall and contains carved limestone seat walls and benches and is flanked by tall flagpoles atop limestone pediments. Live oaks buffer the square from the nearby streets.

HOUSTON CITY HALL

901 Bagby Street

Originally located at Market Square, the hub of Houston activity, city leaders decided a new location was needed for city hall as growth pushed away. Delayed by the Great Depression until 1938, the 1939 Art Deco city hall was completed in twenty months and was flanked by the city library and Sam Houston Coliseum.

Houston City Hall was originally located at Old Market Square. By the 1920s, city leaders had decided that site no longer met their needs and urged the establishment of a civic center around Hermann Square. The Great Depression severely limited that outlook, but city all, constructed over twenty months, rose. *Courtesy of Library of Congress.*

The seventeen-story limestone building sits atop a raised terrace at the northwest end of George and Martha Hermann Square. It's decorated with carved relief panels, thirty friezes and ornate aluminum grills around the entryway. Stretching out front is a reflecting pool and on the front terrace are bronze statues of city founders John Kirby Allen and Augustus Chapman Allen.

Inside, the lobby floor depicts the protective role of government and is bookended above by a mural of zodiac signs and depictions of industry, culture, law and Houston's municipal administration. Grillwork medallions feature historic lawgivers ranging from Moses to Thomas Jefferson. A marble stairway leads from the basement to the third floor with city council chambers in between. Significant modifications were made when an annex was built across the street in the 1970s. Some of those modifications were reversed in 1987, and while the interior continues to be altered, much of the outside remains unchanged.

HUMBLE OIL BUILDING

1212 Main Street

The Humble Oil Company grew out of an investment Ross S. Sterling made in 1909 in an oil field north of Houston. His company's new nine-story Italian Renaissance headquarters was located in downtown's residential neighborhood and opened in 1921. Additions came in 1934, with the seventeen-story Humble Tower annex and again in 1938 and 1947.

The original building features a central court that provides a light shaft extending to the first-floor ceiling. The Humble Tower, home to the ornate Humble Executive Board Room, connects to the original building's center section. The Clay Avenue entrance was remodeled in the 1950s, and in 1963, a pavilion for Air France was added. The company merged with Standard Oil in 1959, moved to a new building in 1963 and dropped the Humble Oil name in 1972 when Exxon Corporation took over. Starting in 2003, the building began a conversion, and it is now a hotel complex featuring a Courtyard by Marriott, a Residence Inn and a SpringHill Suites.

The Humble Oil Building began as a nine-story structure and later expanded with a seventeen-story tower that you see today. In 1932, renovation work included the addition of central air conditioning, the first in any Houston office building. *Author's collection.*

JULIA IDESON LIBRARY BUILDING

500 McKinney Street

Julia Bedford Ideson, head librarian during the Houston Library System's 1904 establishment, saw the need for a new building as early as 1920. Working with a library building committee, Ideson studied U.S. libraries for what constituted good design. Architects created this L-shaped Spanish Renaissance Revival building, which was completed in 1926. Constructed of brick, cast stone and limestone, it features a red Spanish tile roof, an abundance of ornamentation and ornate metalwork.

Searching the exterior, one can find shields for the United States and Texas; cherubs; emblems for France, Spain, Mexico and the Confederacy; reliefs featuring famous explorers; seals for the city, the Houston family and the library; fleurs; an open book; a cow skull; and wreaths. The interior features a red quarry tile lobby on the ground floor, a large oak ceiling, an auditorium, carved built-in bookcases, a tile picture of Don Quixote and multiple murals (added in the 1930s).

Originally set to serve as a prototype for Houston's public buildings, the plan was scrapped when the Great Depression hit. Following Ideson's death in 1945, the city renamed the building in her honor. Over the years, the building was modernized, rooms were reconfigured and a southwest wing was added. A new Central Building, housing administrative and public core

Named for the first head librarian of the Houston Public Library, the Julia Ideson Library Building opened in 1926, supplanting the much smaller Carnegie Library. Today, it is part of the Central Library and is home to the archives, manuscripts, Texas and local history department and the Houston Metropolitan Research Center. *Author's collection.*

services, opened in 1976, and the Ideson Building underwent restoration and renovation work before reopening in 1979 as home to the Houston Metropolitan Research Center.

LEVY BROTHERS DRY GOODS

914 Main Street

The Levy Brothers Dry Goods Company, started in 1887, was once the South's largest mercantile establishment. In 1928, architect Joseph Finger finished the design of a four-story Art Deco building for Abraham and Leo Levy's growing business. However, Jesse Jones hired Alfred Finn to take over prior to construction, adding five floors of office and removing the Art Deco ornamentation.

Completed in 1929, it served as home to the dry goods operation, the chamber of commerce offices, the Houston Club and offices of the United States Department of the Coast Guard Artillery and the 360th Infantry of the United States Army. In 1931, a five-story parking annex was added, and in 1939, the nine-story structure, now known as the United Gas Company Building, grew to twenty-two-stories, while another floor of parking and six floors of office space were added to the annex in 1947. Only the color of brick has revealed any expansion. In the early 1980s, the façade was covered with simple stone panels, though an overhang running the perimeter of the garage annex remained true to the original design. Today, Commerce Tower consists of high-rise luxury apartments.

SAVOY HOTEL

1616–30 Main Street

The seven-story brick Savoy Hotel opened in 1906 and was deemed the tallest in Houston. It is thought to be Houston's first public building with electricity. The Savoy Hotel lasted for three years and, in 1909, was transformed into Houston's first high-rise apartment building. In 1966, a seventeen-story addition was added to the complex. In the late 1980s, the South Texas College of Law took over the building, transforming it into the Barrister Club as student housing. By 1988, the two buildings sat empty, decaying until the roof caved in and bricks were beginning to fall. It was eventually declared structurally unsound. In 2009, the original Savoy Hotel came down, but the 1966 addition remained. It was purchased and fully restored in 2013. After sitting empty for more than two decades, it reopened in 2016 as a Holiday Inn.

THE BEACONSFIELD

1700 Main Street

Multi-unit apartment buildings were still unique when the Beaconsfield opened in late 1910. The eight-story upscale apartment complex housed sixteen units, each with two screened balconies, six large rooms with fireplaces, servants' quarters, elevators, back stairways and parking. They were designed to entice those considering single-family homes.

The building rises in four stages: the first is faced with red-brown brick; the second, containing the first- and second-floor apartments, is painted green-gray; the third is the largest, holding floors three through six, and is faced with tan brick; and the fourth is topped with the main entablature. A detailed parapet peaks above the central bay's arched entry and contains ornamentation with a large identifying *B*.

The building was converted into a modern condominium facility in 1977 with only minor changes to the exterior. Inside, small solariums on the north and south end were converted into closets or mechanical spaces, and the third bedrooms on the upper floors were joined to create smaller efficiency units. Otherwise, much of the building has retained its original appearance.

SAM HOUSTON PARK

1100 Bagby Street

In 1900, Mayor Sam Brashear purchased the Kellum-Noble land and house on the western edge of town, creating Houston's first city park. Covering twenty acres, the city's park committee had it landscaped into a Victorian village featuring footpaths, a small bridge over a stream, the Kellum-Noble House and an old mill. Over the years, features included a bandstand, a children's playground, a wading pond and a nascent version of the Houston Zoo.

Sam Houston Park was the first urban park to be established in the city. The twenty-acre park was landscaped into a Victorian-style village with footpaths leading past an old mill, across a bridge and over a small stream. The park is home to the Heritage Society and several historic homes. *Author's collection.*

In 1954, a group of Houstonians started the Heritage Society. Its purpose continues to be the preservation of the community's history through historic structures, artifacts and programs that focus on Houston and Harris County. Now home to nineteen acres, Sam Houston Park features live oaks, the Heritage Society Museum and eight historic structures dating back to 1823. The following are historic structures that are now located in Sam Houston Park.

BAKER FAMILY PLAYHOUSE

Original Locations: 1104 San Jacinto Street, 1417 Main Street (1904), 22 Courtlandt Place (1918), 207 Bremond (1940), 1216 Bissonet (1940), 1213 Berthea (1946) and Sam Houston Park (2012)

This small playhouse with a front porch has lasted longer than most of its adjacent homes. Captain James A. Baker built the house for his daughter Alice in 1893. Entertaining four generations of Baker children, the playhouse moved with the Baker family five times, first by a horse-drawn cart, then a Model T truck, a couple of times with a small moving van and finally pushed through a hedge from one backyard to the next before finally landing in Sam Houston Park.

One "occupant" of the playhouse was future United States secretary of state James A. Baker, Captain Baker's grandson, who stored elk heads from hunting expeditions in the building. In 2010, the final owner of the structure was redeveloping the property, and the playhouse (then being used as a cabana) needed to be moved. The Heritage Society took over and restored it to its original use, moving it behind the Nichols-Rice-Cherry House for future generations to enjoy.

Fourth Ward Cottage

Original Location: 809 Robin Street

This 1868 cottage was home to a German immigrant family in the middle of the nineteenth century and served as a rental house from 1883 to 2001. By the turn of the twentieth century, the surrounding area had become Freedmen's Town, a major hub for black education, business and culture in Houston.

This home was originally two buildings before they were joined together. A one-room Acadian cottage creates the front portion of the house, and the rear is a two-room cottage, resulting in a shotgun layout that resembles its Robin Street neighbors. Modifications were made over the years and include evidence of a side porch that once ran the entire width of the house and a trap door likely leading to a root cellar.

Kellum-Noble House

Original Location: 212 Dallas Avenue

The Kellum-Noble House sits on its original foundation—the oldest in Houston to do so. Nathaniel Kellum arrived in 1839, starting a brickyard and buying land for his business and a future home. Construction of the white brick house, patterned after Louisiana plantations, began in 1847, with bricks fired at Kellum's brickyard. The two-story, Southern Colonial brick home displays an old Louisiana French influence in its double verandas that are supported by narrow, square brick pillars.

The Kellum-Noble House is Houston's oldest brick home. It was built by Nathaniel Kellum in 1947 out of his own bricks. Kellum operated a brick kiln, tannery and sawmill on the property. The home was later used as one of Houston's first private schools by Mrs. Zerviah Noble. *Courtesy of Library of Congress.*

In 1849, Kellum sold the land, home and brickyard to Abram W. Noble and relocated his growing family near Anderson, Texas. The Nobles moved in, and Abram took over the brickyard while his wife, Zeviah, and their daughter, Catherine, operated one of the area's earliest schools inside the home. Following the Civil War, Abram divorced Zeviah, who retained the house and continued to operate the school until her death in 1894. In developing the city's first public park, Houston used the Kellum-Noble House as its centerpiece, and it once served as the park keeper's residence and headquarters.

NICHOLS-RICE-CHERRY HOUSE

Original Locations: 200 San Jacinto Street, 806 Fargo Street

In 1850, General Ebenezer Nichols built this two-story Greek Revival home, which fronts Courthouse Square's north side. In 1856, he sold the home and his share of a dry goods business to his partner, William Marsh

The Nichols-Rice-Cherry House was built about 1850 and was originally located on San Jacinto Street. Between 1856 and 1873, it was owned by financier William Marsh Rice, whose estate helped create what is now Rice University. *Courtesy of Library of Congress.*

Rice. Rice moved in 1863, following the death of his wife, Margaret, and for the next three decades, the home served as a boardinghouse. The home is made of white pines and hardwood and includes a two-story porch that originally covered three sides. Slaves owned by the Nichols and Rice families lived in an outbuilding either above or adjacent to a detached kitchen.

In danger of being razed, the house went to auction in 1897 with the provision that it be moved. Spurred by admiration for the front door alone, Emma Richardson Cherry won with a twenty-five-dollar bid. Cherry, an artist who would paint murals for the Houston Public Library, moved the house (minus the dining room, kitchen and accessory buildings) to the Montrose area. She added rooms to the back, which would serve as a home and art studio for classes until her death in 1959. The Heritage Society dismantled the home and moved it to the park. Today, it depicts William Marsh Rice's life as one of Houston's wealthiest residents and Cherry's studio.

Pillot House

Original Location: 1803 McKinney Street

Eugene Pillot, a French immigrant to Texas via New York City, was an early Houston homebuilder who operated a lumber business. Pillot developed several properties, including the Pillot Building and the Pillot Opera House. Eugene built this one-story Victorian home in 1868 near present-day Discovery Green, then a residential neighborhood, for his family—his wife, Zeolide, and their six children.

This five-room cottage was one of the first to have an attached kitchen with running water, closets and gas lighting. Highlights include full-length windows and wraparound porches, both designed to temper Houston's hot climate. Guarding the entryway are two large, iron dog statues that are replicas of the damaged originals in the collection. The leaded glass front door incorporates the original street address along the top, and the letter *P* is repeated in flanking windows. Since being moved to Sam Houston Park in 1965, the Pillot home has been relocated and raised several times due to flooding in 1998, 2001 and 2017.

San Felipe Cottage

Original Location: 313 San Felipe Road

The San Felipe Cottage was built in 1868 near what is now the Galleria area. Numerous immigrant families from Germany, Switzerland, Ireland and England called this cottage home, and ownership, due to Texas property rights, passed through the hands of three different women during the 1800s.

The cottage is typical of nineteenth-century East Texas Cottages that Houston's German population lived in. The Greek Revival home features six rooms, a simple gallery across the front and a small dormer balcony above the front door. A miniature staircase rises from the rear gallery to the central hall, leading to two rooms.

Individuals who went on to serve the city as business owners, city council members and city fire chiefs called the cottage home at one time. In 1962, facing demolition, the cottage was moved to Sam Houston Park. It now includes several pieces of Texas-made furniture from the 1870s and showcases the lifestyle of the German working class.

St. John Church

Original Location: Mangum Road and Vista Village Lane

German and Swiss immigrant farmers in northwest Harris County formed an Evangelical Lutheran congregation in Vollmer around 1860. In 1891, they constructed this small church, along with an adjacent school and cemetery, on the upper White Oak Bayou as a replacement for two previous churches.

The Gothic Revival church cost less than $1,000 to build, which left a little extra for the bell and organ. The cypress plank pews were handmade, the shutters were added during the first decade and the interior was painted an umbra white. The pulpit was painted in a black, white and gold schematic and predates this church building.

Services were held primarily in German until the 1930s, evidenced by two Bible verses written in German at either end of the church. By the 1950s, attendance had dwindled, and the church faced closure. The remaining congregants donated the pulpit to a new church, many of the pews were given away and in 1968, the building moved to Sam Houston Park.

Oriented with the altar at the east, the church is situated just as it was on its original site. The flooring is likely original as are the tenon wall glass lights and the organ. The German Bible verses have been refurbished, and the original pulpit and four original pews are back.

Staiti House

Original Location: 421 Westmoreland Street

This California bungalow–style house was originally constructed by E.O. Maynard in 1905 as a speculative house in the Westmoreland neighborhood, one of Houston's earliest subdivisions, located south of downtown. It's typical of an upper-middle-class home in post-oil-boom Houston. The seven-room home was purchased later that year by oil pioneer Henry Thomas Staiti and his wife, Odelia, who came to Houston after he formed his own oil exploration company.

Maynard built the home to accommodate Houston's climate—high ceilings, large windows and broad verandas. A large garage and attached porte cochere were part of the property, as was an intercom system, built-in icebox, electric lighting and a professionally landscaped garden with a sprinkler system.

The house was renovated and expanded in 1915, following significant hurricane damage, and included built-in bookcases, sunrooms on both floors, two sleeping porches, a bathroom across the back and the conversion of a back porch into an informal dining area. Additions included a teahouse and connecting pergola, a greenhouse and a combination chicken house/gardener's cottage. Members of the Staiti family lived in the home until 1980. After a four-year vacancy, and facing demolition, it was donated and moved to Sam Houston Park. Its original home was replaced with two townhomes.

THE OLD PLACE

Original Location: 21410 Gulf Freeway, Webster

Believed to be Harris County's oldest structure, this 1823 log cabin showcases the life and hardships faced by colonial Texas immigrants. John R. Williams originally owned the 1824 cabin, located along the banks of Clear Creek near present-day League City. It changed hands multiple times over the next 150 years and was used by those involved in the cattle industry for much of its early life.

In 1871, Joseph Davis purchased the Old Place, passing it to his daughter, Mary, who eventually passed it to her daughter, whose family ultimately donated it to the Heritage Society. Constructed of roughly hewn cedar logs, this one-room, single-story cabin was eventually encapsulated inside a series of expansions. Covered with cedar clapboard siding, it features a front porch and entry on the west façade. Additions began in the 1850s, and it eventually expanded into a nine-room Victorian cottage.

Restoration work has brought the building back to its original size, sitting atop a pier-and-beam foundation made of tree stumps. The process has uncovered the original lintel, basic frame construction, windowsills and wooden pegs in the walls. A reproduction mudcat chimney and fireplace are located on the north façade, and the porch was rebuilt. Restoration work is ongoing, and in 2010, an outhouse was added.

Yates House

Original Location: 1318 Andrews Street

Following emancipation, Jack Yates relocated his family to Houston—as did many other freed slaves—and became a wagon driver. Because he was literate, he was recruited by the American Baptist Home Mission Society and was ordained to serve as the first pastor of its Antioch Missionary Baptist Church. In 1870, he built this two-story residence for his wife, Harriet, and their family.

Built of cypress in a simplified Greek Revival style, it was in Freedmen's Town and is now furnished to represent the family's lifestyle, including Yates's desk that was fashioned from an old piano. While living here, Yates grew his family, helped establish Emancipation Park in 1872, supervised the church's move to its present location, formed Bethel Baptist Church and helped organize the Houston Academy for Negroes in 1894.

Following his death in 1897, ownership passed in and out of the Yates family's hands before they ultimately donated the house to the Heritage Society in 1994. Over the years, repairs and renovations resulted in the addition of electricity and a kitchen to the back of the house. Using an 1890s photo of the house, the Heritage Society made some alterations during its relocation—round columns became square, a porch and columns were reconstructed and the original floorplan and stairway were restored.

5
FIFTH WARD

T.E. SWANN WAREHOUSE

1011 Wood Street

The Walker-Smith Company, a wholesale grocer, leased a parcel of land in 1915 from the Texas and New Orleans Railroad with the stipulation that a warehouse be built there within sixty days. This two-story, brick and concrete building was the result. Thomas E. Swann, owner of the Talking Machine Company of Texas, purchased the lease and expanded with this adjacent warehouse in 1923.

Standing three stories high, it resembles its shorter neighbor, featuring a similar brick, wood and steel construction. Swann sold his company, moved his family back to Tyler, Texas, shortly after completing the building and leased it to the Reichardt Electric Company, which remained until 1942. In later years, Central Supply Electric Company and the Day Furniture Company resided in the building. It has since been renovated for use as offices on the first floor and luxury apartments above.

PEDEN COMPANY BUILDING

600–610 North San Jacinto Street

After entering the hardware and mill supply business in 1890, Edward Andrew Steel later formed Smith, Peden and Co. with his father and brother. The company served as a wholesale supply house for hardware, iron and steel, railways, mills and oil wells and grew with markets in San Antonio, Shreveport and Mexico.

Its first building rose on the south side of the bayou on Travis Street in 1890 and followed with another in 1905. In 1929, needing a center for its retail store and administration offices, the group built this four-story modernistic building on the north side of Buffalo Bayou, with lower levels accessible to barge traffic along the bayou.

Warehouses moved structural steel such as H-beams, channel iron, steel plating, mechanical tubing, drill stem pipe and valves. If a hardware store in Texas sold something, it likely came from a Peden warehouse. Peden warehouses were loaded with products as varied as kitchen utensils, guns, jeans, baseballs, nails and even lion repellent. After the company was sold in the 1970s, it only survived a short time before closing. Harris County purchased this building and currently uses it is County Annex no. 27 and a county correctional facility.

WILLOW STREET PUMP STATION

811 North San Jacinto

Located near the confluence of White Oak and Buffalo Bayous, the Willow Street Pump Station was an integral part of Houston's first wastewater system. As the city evolved, locals grew tired of the polluted bayous and inefficient wastewater treatment system. When the federal government threatened to withhold Houston Ship Channel funding, progress finally came.

Alexander Potter designed the brick Romanesque Revival pump station and nearby storage building. Built directly on the banks of White Oak Bayou in 1902, it sits lower than the larger storage building and is connected by a steep staircase. Both feature arched windows and a large arched door. The station featured a unique pumping system that separated storm water through large pipes with the sewage passing through smaller clay pipes. The effluent was then pumped through a three-layered filtration system.

The complex was expanded in later years; a one-story brick and concrete incinerator was added in 1914. Another was added in 1924 (since removed) and a grit chamber for larger debris filtration was added in 1930. By the 1980s, the station was obsolete and sat abandoned for years until the University of Houston began rehabbing and repurposing it as an education facility. A portion of the site has been left undeveloped due to regular flooding.

SOUTHERN PACIFIC LINES FREIGHT DEPOT

810 North San Jacinto Street

This two-story warehouse was designed in-house by R.W. Barnes, chief engineer for the freight depot of the Southern Pacific's Houston office. Constructed in 1928, the concrete frame and brick infill warehouse branches out on a diagonal from the Houston and Texas Central's transfer track.

Southern Pacific Railroad became firmly entrenched in this part of Houston by 1881, absorbing the Texas and New Orleans, the Houston and Texas Central and the Houston East and West Texas lines. Today it serves the Harris County sheriff's office as its support services building.

FIFTH WARD HOTEL

814 Walnut Street/1206 Nance Street

When finished in 1883, the three-story Fifth Ward Hotel was the only hotel north of Buffalo Bayou. Strategically located near the large railyards, it featured a series of tenants, a billiard hall, saloon and dry goods store, in a portion of the first floor. The hotel layout was "conducted to the American and European plans," meaning it housed both private and shared baths. Connected directly to Buffalo Bayou, it quickly became an attractive magnet for many nearby railroad workers.

The hotel underwent several name changes, first as the Fifth Ward Hotel until 1900, followed by the Hotel Belknap, Brooklyn Hotel, Phoenix and briefly the Liberty until 1927. It then stood vacant until the 1930s, when Mrs. Margie Daugherty began providing furnished rooms to let and leasing out the ground floor to dry goods merchants, the Southwestern Bag Company, a wholesale confectioners and candy manufacturer and a furniture merchant. In the 1950s, the building received extensive renovations, including complete removal of the upper two floors and a sheet metal covering on the first-floor façade, which was finally removed at the turn of the century.

HENRY HENKE'S FIFTH WARD GROCERY

1200 Rothwell (Nance) Street

Henry Henke was a young grocer in 1872. Operating his business in New Orleans, Henry decided to take a short vacation to Galveston, hoping to form a partnership with a fellow grocer who was just starting out. When the partnership didn't come to fruition, Henke traveled on to Houston, deciding to make a go of it in a town full of competitors.

This four-story, low-rise commercial building in the Fifth Ward served as Henke's New Orleans Store from 1883 until 1884. That year, Henke hired Camille Pillot to run his books, later bringing him into full partnership as Henke and Pillot. This building continued to house grocery operations until 1901, when it began hosting a variety of restaurants and saloons for the next twenty-five years. From the late 1920s to the late 1970s, it was home to the North San Jacinto Café.

BUTE COMPANY WAREHOUSE

711 William Street

James Bute founded his paint company in 1867, growing it into one of the largest paint companies in the country. In 1910, James Bute Paints and Oils built what was the city's largest warehouse at the time—a four-story, simple red-brick building. It's still one of the tallest buildings in the warehouse district.

Sitting adjacent to the Houston East and West Texas Railway tracks, the utilitarian building's two sprinkler system water tanks rest atop the building's penthouse, serving as landmarks. The brick exterior showcases the historic business's purpose and ranges in color from orange to deep purple. The Bute Paint Company operated until 1990 and is believed to be the longest continually operating business in the city's history. Three years later, the warehouse was converted into loft apartments in one of Houston's first urban renewal projects. Today, it houses a mix of residential lofts and business studios.

ERIE CITY IRON WORKS WAREHOUSE

1302 Nance Street

Located in the warehouse district, the Erie City Iron Works warehouse was built by Herbert A. Paine to house his wholesale machinery business and showroom. As Houston began transitioning from masonry to iron and steel construction, many of the materials being used passed through this warehouse. Supplies came in on rail lines that still exist today, lightly buried under the asphalt of Sterret Street.

Paine's brown brick warehouse has changed little since its completion in 1909, aside from some modernization. Today, the warehouse is home to artists, chefs and loft residents.

LAST CONCERT CAFE

1403 Nance Street

Immortalized in Larry McMurtry's *Terms of Endearment*, the Last Concert Café is well known for its food, music and anonymity. The complex wasn't even marked by name until recently. Before that, you just had to know it was there, and even then, you had to knock twice and be approved for entry.

Elena Aldrete "Mama" Lopez sold her jewelry to construct her enterprise, opening her cafe in 1949—the first post–World War II restaurant owned by a woman. The one-story, Spanish-style, stucco café is white and features red tile trim, an arched entryway, small windows, glass blocks and flower boxes running along the front. The patio, enclosed by a long red fence, includes a six-room home constructed in 1850 and a two-room servant's quarters—both rumored as former brothels but used today as a kitchen facility, dining hall and offices.

The Last Concert Café has been an under-the-radar institution in Houston, serving Mexican food and music since the 1940s. There is no sign, and visitors used to have to knock and be allowed to enter—something that wasn't always a certainty. It gained a bit more fame after being included in Larry McMurtry's novel *Terms of Endearment. Author's collection.*

Inside, the original bar, faced in glass blocks, is a painted brick wall—a mix of aquamarine, purple, light lavender and light machinery gray. The only major changes came in the 1980s when the kitchen was enlarged into the old garage area and a stage was added.

6
SIXTH WARD

HOUSTON FIRE STATION NO. 1/CENTRAL WATERWORKS

400 Bagby Street

Originally, this was the site of Houston's Fire Station No. 1 and the Central Waterworks plant. By 1999, the city was ready to unload these properties and put out a request for proposals for the redevelopment of the two sites. The following year, locally owned Landry's won the competition to redevelop the site. The Central Waterworks plant was transformed into a shark and stingray exhibition habitat. The main restaurant was on the second floor of the old firehouse and the rest of the aquarium exhibits were downstairs. While much of the building was removed, the basic framework of the fire station and much of the waterworks plant were kept intact while construction took place. The aquarium opened in 2003, and while little is left of the fire station, the waterworks plant remains similar in appearance.

PART II

HOUSTON'S WARDS

1

FIRST WARD

L ooking at a map of the ward system, we start in the northwest quadrant with the First Ward. It was originally the center of Houston's business district. Located near what is now Allen's Landing, it sits at the confluence of Buffalo Bayou and White Oak Bayou, encompassing the area north of Congress and west of Main.

Economically, the base of the First Ward was primarily industrial with rail service and water access dominating the area. Land that wasn't taken over by industry was used primarily for farming. The bayous made the area a natural choice for the city's first port, with rail service, produce merchants and shipping filling up commercial enterprises. Commerce Street, the road closest to the docks, became known as Produce Row. The economic makeup changed little during the life of the ward; however, when a massive hurricane hit Galveston in 1900, it was decided that there was a need for a larger inland port, and a few years later, the port was moved several miles seaward.

In 1866, the land to the north and east of White Oak Bayou and Little White Oak Bayou was carved off to create the Fifth Ward. Today, the First Ward area located in downtown has fully adapted and changed with the times. It thrives but does include remnants of its former ward life. Outside of its downtown confines, the First Ward is primarily an arts district that includes a handful of remaining nineteenth- and early twentieth-century bungalows and cottages as part of the High First Ward Historic District.

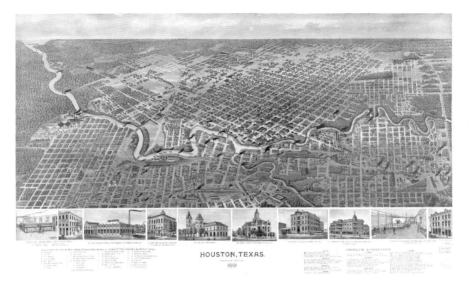

Bird's-eye view maps, like this one of Houston looking south in 1891, were all the rage in the late nineteenth century. They featured various important landmarks and buildings with directories of public buildings, hotels, railroads, churches and more at the bottom of the page. *Courtesy of Library of Congress.*

FIRE STATION NO. 3

1919 Houston Avenue

Organized in 1867, Stonewall No. 3 was originally located on Travis Street where the rear portion of the Rice Hotel now sits. The fire company moved to a new building on Preston Street in 1895 before moving to this two-story brick building in 1903. The company remained in this building until 1937 and has since been in two additional buildings. This building underwent massive restoration work in 2014. The project kept the original brick, wood floors, concrete beams and exterior hand-carved stonework. The motto "Trust in Us" is still etched into the building's intricately carved stone. Today, it operates as a special event venue and has been listed by the city and state as a historic landmark.

HOLLYWOOD CEMETERY

3506 North Main Street

Covering fifty-five acres and holding more than thirty-four thousand graves, Hollywood Cemetery did *not* get its name from the movie location in California. Instead, the cemetery, founded in 1895, got its name from a family who the original founders of the property admired. Dedicated as a "garden of rest," the cemetery is located on a portion of land granted to John Austin in 1824. The first interment took place the year after its founding. In 1926, the cemetery was bought by Thomas C. Hall, and its operation stayed in the family until 1994. It served as the primary graveyard for the white residents of Houston Heights.

By the 1970s, as demographics of the area changed, most burials were of nearby Latino residents. Some of the more notable burials include Mollie Arline Kirkland, civil war nurse, spy in Hood's Texas Brigade and Bailey Circus co-owner; Julia Ideson, Houston's pioneering librarian and civic activist; Lawrence Shipley, of famed Shipley Donuts; Andrew George Simmons, the inventor of the ice cream cone; and many other Texas Republic descendants, celebrities, government officials and soldiers. It remains an active cemetery.

HIGH FIRST WARD HISTORIC DISTRICT

Crockett Street and surrounding arteries

The High First Ward was historically a working-class neighborhood. Settlers included immigrants from a variety of locations. Just outside downtown, but still close to Market Square, Buffalo Bayou and two rail lines, the First Ward was a major player for the shipment of goods, and many of the residents worked in positions that served these industries. Today, the High First Ward hosts a number of Queen Anne cottages and Craftsman bungalows that were constructed between 1890 and 1930—many of them modest in scale and design. It became a City of Houston historic district in 2014.

2

SECOND WARD

Extending from the center of downtown Houston eastward to the city limits is Houston's Second Ward, one of the city's original four wards. Considered to be one of the city's most culturally significant neighborhoods, the heart of the area during the twentieth century is most closely identified with the area bound by Buffalo Bayou to the north, downtown to the west and the Houston Belt and Terminal Railways to the south and east. The area's historic significance spans Houston's life, holding a number of Houston's original recorded deeds and becoming a focal point in the city's twentieth-century industrial expansion.

For many today, the Second Ward identifies with Latino culture, though the neighborhood has hosted a variety of settlements from different ethnic groups. During the mid- to late nineteenth century, the area was inhabited largely by German settlers. Later, the neighborhood was popular with Italians and Anglos, and by the 1920s, the Latino community began growing. During this time, the area was settled primarily by those of Mexican origin but has since become much more diverse, with the population now peppered with those from Mexico as well as Central America.

Houston's Missouri, Kansas, Texas (MKT) Freight Terminal stands as a historic symbol not only for the growth of Houston's rail industry but also for the growth of its surrounding neighborhoods in the 1920s. Employees chose to work nearby, thus influencing the early development of suburbs, the city's port and the evolution of Houston as not only a regional but also a national transportation center. MKT is known colloquially as "the Katy," which influenced the name for Houston's suburb of Katy, Texas. *Courtesy of Library of Congress.*

Our Sister of Guadalupe Church, constructed in 1911, was the first Mexican American church in Houston and the first in the city to offer religious services in Spanish. It also opened one of the first schools for Mexican American children. The current church building was constructed in 1923. *Author's collection.*

MAGNOLIA PARK CITY HALL AND CENTRAL FIRE STATION

7301 Avenue F

Remnants of the city of Magnolia Park, one of Houston's oldest Latino neighborhoods, are few. Its former fire station/city hall structure is the only municipal structure remaining. Constructed in 1923, the combination city hall/fire station structure, with attached calaboose serving as the city jail, was a popular 1920s trend (a similar one exists in the Heights). Taking the place of the original fire station, it was situated next to the city's water and natural gas plants and was flanked on the west by the Houston Belt and Terminal Railway and the Galveston, Harrisburg, and San Antonio Railway to the east. It served the city of Magnolia Park for only two years.

When Magnolia Park and Houston voters approved annexation into Houston in 1926, ownership of the building transferred, and it became Houston Fire Station No. 20 until 1973. It handled chemical spills and fires along the Houston Ship Channel, while the jail became a police substation. After the fire department moved into a new station in 1973, the building was vacated. Today, it serves as a Harris County polling place and offices for community service programs.

Magnolia Park Scene, Houston, Texas.

Located near the Houston Ship Channel, Magnolia Park is one of the oldest Latino neighborhoods in the city. There are many historical buildings throughout Magnolia Park, especially along Harrisburg and Canal Street. *Courtesy of Special, University of Houston Libraries.*

IMMACULATE CONCEPTION CATHOLIC CHURCH

7250 Harrisburg Boulevard

The oblates of Mary Immaculate established their first parish in October 1911, naming it the Immaculate Conception and locating it in Magnolia Park. The following year, they dedicated a three-building campus that included a wood frame church, school, boardinghouse and rectory. In 1936, a consolidated brick school and auditorium, which also served as the church, replaced the original facilities. The 1912 church building was relocated two miles away and converted into a brick building to serve another parish. The 1936 school and auditorium received a complementary Neo-Romanesque church building in 1957. By 1969, the boardinghouse had ceased operations, and the school was closed permanently. However, the church building continues to operate in the Magnolia Park neighborhood.

SOCIEDAD MUTUALISA OBRERA MEXICANA (SMOM) BUILDING

5804 Canal Street

From its construction in 1946 through the 1950s, this Art Moderne stucco building housed Model Pharmacy and was owned by barber Joseph Sills. A second storefront occupied by Pipe Fitters Local Union No. 211 gives its historical importance. Until 1978, the Seafarers International Union of North America and Marine Engineers Beneficial Association occupied the space. It was later replaced by Sociedad Mutualista Obrera Mexicana (SMOM).

SMOM began in 1932 to help Houstonians with Mexican heritage in times of trouble, assisting financially with medical emergencies and funeral expenses. While apolitical in membership and limited to men, wives and daughters were heavily involved in the society's activities. As the organization grew, it sought out this location as the permanent offices. Opening to Norwood and Canal Streets, the building represents the East End commercial and industrial development of the post–World War II era. The two-storefront building was remodeled into one unit during the 1960s, and a major 1990s renovation restored the first floor's appearance and converted the second-floor union hall to a rental space.

CONTINENTAL CAN COMPANY BUILDING

5900 Canal Street

Located across the street from SOMA is the Continental Can Company Building, home to *The Rebirth of Our Nationality*, once the city's largest mural. Painted by Leo Tanguma, the mural covers four thousand square feet and stretches the full block. The painting depicts the Chicano movement and has been an artistic icon in the East End since it was completed. Harris County purchased the factory building in 2012 for use as the office of Harris County Precinct 6 constable's staff and a records storage facility. Local muralist Gonzo 247 was chosen to restore the mural and did so under the direction and assistance of the original artist in 2018. The mural features seventy distinct characters illustrates a narrative of Mexican Americans throughout the twentieth century, including laborers, union activists, soldiers, farm workers, prisoners and families.

ST. VINCENT DE PAUL CEMETERY

2400 Navigation Boulevard

Established by the St. Vincent de Paul Catholic Church in 1853, this was the first Catholic cemetery in Houston. In an area settled by a diverse range of immigrants, headstones can be found carved with French, German and Spanish surnames, among others. Buried here are Confederate lieutenant

Saint Vincent de Paul Cemetery was established by the St. Vincent de Paul Catholic Church in 1853. Headstones feature a melting pot of nationalities. Interred here is Dick Dowling, the "Hero of the Battle of Sabine Pass" during the Civil War. *Author's collection.*

Richard "Dick" Dowling, considered to be the hero of the Civil War's Battle of Sabine Pass; John Kennedy, a merchant who ran Kennedy's Trading Post (now La Carafe) on old Market Square in downtown; and Samuel Paschall, a private during the Battle of San Jacinto. Also interred are numerous victims of the yellow fever epidemics during the early to mid-1800s, as well as numerous unmarked grave sites

The cemetery was condemned by the City of Houston, partly because of its burials of yellow fever victims in 1867. Hurricanes in 1900 and 1915 damaged many of the cemetery's markers. Today, the cemetery sits adjacent to Our Lady of Guadalupe Church and has been inactive for several years. An arch over the primary entryway was erected in 1947 to mark the cemetery's historical significance.

3
THIRD WARD

Located in the southeast quadrant is the Third Ward, immediately southeast of downtown and east of the Texas Medical Center. Nicknamed the Tre, it became the heart of Houston's African American community. It originally extended south of Congress Street and east of Main Street, ending at Brays Bayou.

During the nineteenth century, much of the Third Ward was an elite neighborhood filled with Victorian-era homes. However, when the construction of Union Station arrived in 1910, the residential character of the area shifted to commercial, and new hotels, stores and theaters opened. As passenger trains dwindled and then quit coming to Union Station altogether, those hotels turned into flophouses, buildings were torn down and commercial operations went bust and closed up shop, causing the area to deteriorate by the 1990s.

White citizens lived in the southern part of the ward while African Americans lived north of Truxillo Street. After World War II, white residents began moving to new suburbs on the southwest side and the demographics of the ward became predominately African American.

During segregation, Almeda Road, which served as a feeder road to downtown, became a busy commercial corridor, while the construction of I-45 in the 1950s separated the area and visually moved boundaries into downtown and cut off the rest of the ward. Throughout the rest of the twentieth century, the Third Ward experienced an exodus of its residents to southwestern suburbs, such as Missouri City. Additional construction, such

Built by the Houston Belt and Terminal Railway Company, the construction of Union Station cleared a large portion of residential homes located on the east end of downtown. Union Station has been incorporated into Minute Maid Park. *Courtesy of Library of Congress.*

as that of Highway 288, further divided the ward, tossing it into disarray with drugs and violence becoming synonymous with the area. Since the beginning of the twenty-first century, residents looking for cheaper housing and development opportunities close to downtown began moving into the ward. Gentrification has become more noticeable, and the area has continued redevelopment as more attention has been given to Midtown, East Downtown, the Museum District and the surrounding areas.

ST. JOHN MISSIONARY BAPTIST CHURCH

2222 Gray Street

An institution within Houston's African American community since 1899, several churches have housed the congregation over the years. A split in the congregation in 1916 and 1917 led to the creation of two separate congregations—one located in a small building owned by Trinity Methodist Episcopal Church (now located at 2702 Emancipation Avenue), while the rest remained here. Although the new congregation was considerably larger at the time of the split, the St. John assembly grew quickly, necessitating a new building by the end of World War II.

This new three-story Gothic Revival church building was constructed in 1946 by James Thomas, a black contractor who specialized in churches. The nave was elevated above a raised basement, and its two towers were a style favored by local African American congregations at the time. As the building went up, the congregation continued to grow. In 1952, it numbered nearly five thousand worshippers.

CONGREGATION BETH ISRAEL

3517 Austin Street

Founded in 1854 and chartered in 1859, the Orthodox Beth Israel congregation in Houston began in a home converted into a synagogue. In 1874, it was converted to Reform Judaism and completed the Franklin Avenue Temple in what is now downtown Houston. The congregation later moved and occupied a new temple at Crawford and Lamar, in an area that was a Jewish community. A new Moderne-style temple was dedicated in 1925 and features a mix of traditional classical and near eastern elements.

By the early 1960s, Houston's Jewish community was steadily moving southwest to Meyerland. The congregation followed and moved to a new temple in 1967, after selling the Austin Street temple the year before to the Houston Independent School District (HISD). Initially, HISD used the temple building as an annex for the growing San Jacinto High School, but it become the first home to Houston's High School for the Performing and Visual Arts (HSPVA) and later became a performance venue, renamed the Heinen Theatre, for Houston Community College.

TRINITY EPISCOPAL CHURCH

1015 Holman Street

Designed to resemble a medieval parish church, the Neo-Gothic Trinity Episcopal Church soars above its neighbors with a ninety-seven-foot-high tower. It began as a cottage mission of Christ Church in 1893 in response to residential growth along Main Street, an area to the southwest known as the

Fairground Addition. Services and classes initially took place in members' parlors and a rented schoolhouse until September 1897, when the mission dedicated its first building.

This first building was a small wooden chapel, but it was moved to its present location in 1910, and a new building opened in 1921. By the 1940s, Trinity Episcopal Church was the largest church in the Episcopal Diocese of Texas and the nation's sixth-largest Episcopal parish.

CHEEK-NEAL COFFEE BUILDING

2017 Preston Street

This five-story, red-brick building was constructed for the growing coffee business of Joel Owsley Cheek and John William Neal, who had developed the famous Maxwell House coffee brand at headquarters in Nashville. From 1917 to 1946, the building was used to manufacture Cheek-Neal's Maxwell House Coffee, though Cheek and Neal sold the brand to Kraft Foods in 1928. They continued to roast, blend, package and ship their coffee across the nation. The company moved to a new Houston facility in 1946, and the building was used by two rubber companies, a furniture business and a floor coverings business before it was abandoned. The most iconic feature is its rooftop water tower, which was replaced with a fiberglass imitation in the early 2000s. Instead of holding a reserve of water, today it hides cellular equipment.

ELDORADO BALLROOM

2310 Elgin Street

The Eldorado billed itself as the "home of Happy Feet" and bridged generational differences, drawing crowds from those in their early twenties to those in their fifties. While many dance halls served food and drinks, the focus of the Eldorado was as a high-class dance venue. It occupied the Eldorado Building's entire second floor and was considered to be the focal point of the Third Ward. Performers such as Louis Armstrong, Sam "Lightnin'" Hopkins, Johnny "Guitar "Watson, Duke Ellington, Count Basie, Della Reese, James Brown, Little Richard, Fats Domino and B.B. King played at

From its opening in 1939 until the early 1970s, the Eldorado was the place to see upscale blues and jazz performances, local talent and events. Performers such as Arnett Cobb, Conrad Johnson, Ray Charles, Etta James, Big Joe Turner and T-Bone Walker were featured at this prestigious landmark. *Author's collection.*

the Eldorado. Business and popularity waned during the 1960s and '70s, and it eventually closed. In 1999, the building and a seventeen-lot block was donated to Project Row Houses to find a connection between the work of artists and the revitalization of the community. To this day, it is a space for music, dancing and community activity. A Texas historical marker highlights the building.

FRANKLIN BEAUTY SCHOOL

3402 Dowling Street

Following years of creating and selling beauty products from her San Antonio home, Nobia Franklin put up her shingle and started the Franklin Beauty School in 1917. A few moves over the years led her to Houston and then Chicago. When Nobia died, her daughter inherited the business and moved it back to Houston in 1935. Though it was first located downtown, as the salon grew, it ended up here.

It was one of the first private cosmetology schools to receive a license in Texas, opening doors for numerous women to pursue professional careers as trained and skilled beauticians at a time when jobs were essentially limited to domestic, field or factory work. Eventually, a second campus was opened, and while the location has changed, it remains in family hands and continues to operate.

HOUSTON NEGRO HOSPITAL/RIVERSIDE GENERAL HOSPITAL

3204 Ennis Street

Houston's first hospital to serve black patients opened in 1911 with six beds in a remodeled house and limited equipment. A new, larger hospital was under construction in 1925 to serve the growing city, opening to patients in the spring of 1927.

The dedication of the Houston Negro Hospital was held on June 19, 1926, a holiday known as Juneteenth that commemorates the day emancipation occurred in Texas. The hospital buildings are listed on the National Register of Historic Places, and it continues to operate today. *Courtesy of Special Collections, University of Houston Libraries.*

The three-story Spanish Colonial Revival building was the first nonprofit hospital in Houston for black patients. It provided stable work for black physicians who were not allowed to admit patients in the black wards of other Houston hospitals. The entire staff was African American, a rarity at the time. Next to the hospital, the Houston Negro Hospital Nursing School, the first of its kind in Houston, opened in 1931. The building was remodeled between 1949 and 1952. A new wing was added, and the complex was renamed Riverside General Hospital in 1961. It underwent more remodeling throughout the 1980s before closing in April 2015. It has since been purchased by Harris County and has been revived as a mental health facility.

JACK YATES SENIOR HIGH SCHOOL

2610 Elgin Street

Established as the Yates Colored High School, the second Houston school for African Americans opened in 1926. In 1927, the Yates building began housing the Houston Colored Junior College, later known as the Houston College for Negroes and now known as Texas Southern University. The student population continued to grow, necessitating an annex in 1955 and prompting the opening of Worthing High School in 1958. That same year, Yates High School moved to a new building on Sampson, with Ryan Colored Junior High School opening in its place. Yates was desegregated by 1970, and after the 2012–13 school year it closed before reopening as the Baylor College of Medicine. Notable alumni of Yates High School include actresses Debbie Allen and Phylicia Rashad; football players Johnny Bailey, Reggie Phillips, Elvis Patterson, Dexter Manley and Jerald Moore; NBA players Michael Young and Rickie Winslow; and Texas state representative Garnet Coleman.

TRINITY UNITED METHODIST CHURCH

2600 Holman Street

Established as a slave congregation in 1848, Trinity UMC holds services to this day and is one of Houston's oldest African American churches—and

Olivewood Cemetery is Houston's first incorporated African American cemetery. Established in 1875, and covering eight acres, time eventually took its toll on the cemetery. Volunteers have cleared out the vegetation, restored the grounds and maintained the historic cemetery. It has been recognized by UNESCO as a significant historic site of memory and is on its Slave Route Project. *Author's collection.*

the first brick one. Originally, the congregation was the slave membership of the Houston Methodist Church. It was given a sanctuary of its own around 1851 and was organized in 1865.

Members of the congregation went on to help establish, among others, Wiley College in 1873, Olivewood Cemetery, Emancipation Park, the Texas Conference, the Freedmen's Aid Society and Houston Colored Junior College in 1925. The current sanctuary was erected in 1951. Visitors to the church will find a set of large stained-glass windows that depict religious and civil rights themes, including scenes from the Old and New Testaments, a black Methodist theme, the Holy Trinity, the Civil War and the Twenty-Fourth Infantry—famed from the 1917 Houston Riot. An offshoot, Trinity East United Methodist Church, served the Third Ward beginning in the early twentieth century.

PROJECT ROW HOUSES

2521 Holman Street

Located within one of the city's oldest African American neighborhoods, Project Row Houses covers five city blocks and houses thirty-nine structures. These buildings serve as a home to a variety of community enrichment initiatives, art programs and neighborhood development activities that engage neighbors, artists and enterprises with an emphasis on cultural identity and how that impacts the urban landscape. Renovation work began in 1993 when seven artists saw the potential in a block and a half of rundown 1930s shotgun houses at the corner of Holman and Live Oak and began exploring how to transform them into a community resource tool and an engine for social transformation.

The homes have been rehabilitated for a multitude of purposes, and along with new construction, they show small, affordable and sustainable housing that is complementary to the historic homes and is open to visitors.

In poor condition by the 1990s, twenty-two shotgun homes built in the 1930s were purchased by a coalition of artists and transformed into Project Row Houses. A shotgun house is a narrow rectangular residence, usually no more than twelve feet wide, with rooms arranged one behind the other and doors at each end of the house. They were the most popular style of house in the South from the end of the Civil War through the 1920s. *Author's collection.*

UNIVERSITY OF HOUSTON

4800 Calhoun Road

Hearing that the third-largest university in Texas is the University of Houston—sliding in just behind Texas A&M and University of Texas with forty-six thousand students—generally surprises people. This 667-acre campus is the main institution of the University of Houston system. It was founded in 1927 as Houston Junior College and was operated and administrated by Houston Independent School District.

Originally located at San Jacinto High School, the junior college offered only night courses. In 1934, the school became a four-year college, renamed University of Houston. It continued operating at San Jacinto High School and then moved to two church locations before its new stand-alone campus opened in September 1939. Since that time, the university has added several buildings and degree programs and has established KUHT—the first public television station in the nation. The campus includes green spaces, fountains and sculptures. Renowned architects have added to the built landscape, and the campus recently added a new football stadium and basketball fieldhouse. Famous alumni include Jack Valenti, longtime president of the Motion Picture Association of America; hip hop artist Lil Wayne; actors Jim Parson and Dennis and Randy Quaid; comedian Bill Hicks; novelist Alice Sebold; presidential candidate and senator Elizabeth Warren; and scores of NFL, MLB, NBA players and Olympians.

EMANCIPATION PARK

3018 Emancipation Avenue

President Lincoln's Emancipation Proclamation freeing slaves in the South was issued on January 1, 1863. With the Civil War still raging, notification of the action didn't reach Texas until June 19, 1865, when General Gordon Granger proclaimed it in Galveston. Over the next few years, African Americans across Texas collected money to buy property that could be dedicated to hosting anniversary traditions to celebrate their freedom, what would become known as Juneteenth.

In Houston, efforts were led by Reverend Jack Yates. His Antioch Baptist Church partnered with Trinity Methodist Episcopal Church to form the Colored People's Festival and Emancipation Park Association. In 1872, this group purchased ten acres of open land, naming it Emancipation Park.

By the time the City of Houston acquired the park in 1918, racial segregation was in full force, and the park was the only one African Americans could use. In 1939, the Works Progress Administration built a community center building and added the adjacent Finnigan Park, donated by and named for suffragette Annette Finnigan. Additions and renovations came in 1976, the 1990s and 2017.

BUFFALO SOLDIERS MUSEUM

3816 Caroline Street

Founded in 2001 by Vietnam veteran and military historian Paul Matthews, this museum chronicles the African American military experience from the Revolutionary War to modern day. Exhibits include uniforms, firearms, photos, documents, military memorabilia and flags. In November 2012, the museum relocated to the Houston Light Guard Armory, a twenty-three-thousand-square-foot building. The armory was built in 1925 and served as headquarters to the Houston Light Guards, one of the oldest National Guard companies in Texas.

TEXAS SOUTHERN UNIVERSITY

3100 Cleburne Street

In 1927, during segregation, the Houston Independent School District resolved to establish junior colleges—one for white students and one for black students. What started as Houston Junior College later transformed into the University of Houston and Houston Colored Junior College before becoming Houston College for Negroes (1934–1947) and finally Texas Southern University.

In the spring of 1945, HISD severed its relationship with Houston College for Negroes, and the college formed a board of regents. In the fall of 1946, the college moved from the high school to the T.M. Fairchild Building, which is still in use today. In 1947, while unsuccessfully fighting the separate but equal doctrine, the college was transformed into a university with the creation of a law school for black students. From this, it became Texas State University for Negroes (1947–51), and following a petition to remove the phrase "for Negroes," it became Texas Southern University. Today, the university serves more than 9,500 students that represent an ethnically and culturally diverse student body.

4

FOURTH WARD

Houston's Fourth Ward, situated west of downtown, became a primary settling place for the city's African American population. Home to Freedmen's Town, this community of freed slaves moved into the area following the Civil War and created one of the largest and strongest African American communities in the state—if not the nation. Unfortunately, this is one of the least preserved areas in the city. With increasing population and shifting demographics, the area has seen constant development.

The first freed slaves left the Brazos River cotton plantations in 1866, entering Houston from the southwest via the San Felipe Road. Settling on the southern edge of the bayou, they built small shanties, used brush arbors and borrowed churches as their places of worship. Nearly one thousand freed slaves settled in this new community, partly because it was inexpensive but also because no one else wanted it—it was prone to flooding and consistently swampy. The settlers paved the streets with handmade bricks and provided their own services and utilities. You could find any service you needed, as residents included everything from blacksmiths to doctors and brickmakers to lawyers. From 1905 through the 1940s, this was where Houstonians—black and white—went to catch baseball games. At West End Park, you could watch the Houston Buffaloes, the city's minor-league team, and later Negro Major League baseball games.

By the 1920s and '30s, the ward's population was nearly six times that of the entire city of Houston, but it began to dwindle as the Third Ward supplanted it as the center of the African American community. Eventually, the ward could no longer expand geographically. Interstate 45, the construction of the all-white San Felipe Courts public housing and the redevelopment of downtown started to cut away at the Fourth Ward, and residents moved away. Rolling into the twenty-first century, the area underwent gentrification with new apartment complexes and upscale townhomes being built, resulting in the loss of many of the original homes. As the area began to draw attention from developers, efforts were made to salvage what remained of the ward's original identity. Today, much of the area has been transformed, but there are still pockets of preserved historic sections of the Fourth Ward.

LULAC COUNCIL 60 CLUBHOUSE

3004 Bagby Street

This 1907 two-story stucco building is now abandoned but served as the League of United Latin American Citizens (LULAC) de facto national headquarters in the 1950s and '60s. Formed in Corpus Christi in 1929, it intended to unifying statewide efforts in combating racism and inequities toward Texas's Latino residents while also promoting patriotism, education and equality. Its efforts sought to improve employment for Mexican Americans, open opportunities within the city and begin what would become Project Head Start, SER-Jobs for Progress and a national housing commission.

It was to Houston's LULAC council that First Lady Jacqueline Kennedy, introduced by her husband, gave an address in Spanish at the Rice Hotel the day before President Kennedy's assassination in Dallas. Now declared a National Treasure, preservation work is currently underway to open the clubhouse to the public.

FOUNDERS MEMORIAL CEMETERY

1217 West Dallas Street

Founded in 1836 as City Cemetery, the two-acre site is now owned and operated by the Houston Parks and Recreation Department. It features many graves from citizens of the Republic of Texas, including John Kirby Allen

Founders Memorial Cemetery is the oldest cemetery in Houston, founded as City Cemetery in 1836. It is the final resting place of Houston cofounder John Kirby Allen and several veterans of the Texas Revolution. By 1840, the cemetery was nearly full, and another city cemetery was created at the present site of Jefferson Davis Hospital. It was restored in 1936 and was officially renamed Founders Memorial Park. *Author's collection.*

(cofounder of Houston), and numerous veterans of the Texas Revolution. It lies adjacent to the oldest Jewish cemetery in Texas, Beth Israel. It contains the second-highest number of Texas Centennial Monuments, after the Texas State Cemetery in Austin.

HOUSTON FIRE MUSEUM

2403 MILAM STREET

At the turn of the twentieth century, what is now Midtown Houston, was once a posh neighborhood on the southern outskirts of downtown. As commercial enterprises swallowed up the residential areas of downtown, the neighborhood residents sought residential space on its edges. Originally protected by volunteer firefighters, the city decided to consolidate and operate its own fire service following a bout of fires that uncovered the growing ineffectiveness of its current model. The city took over the volunteer

Now home to the Houston Fire Museum, Station No. 7, was the first station built for Houston's paid fire service in 1898. It was active until 1969, when it could no longer adequately house new fire vehicles, and a replacement was needed. *Author's collection.*

service, its equipment, most of the staff and station houses. Growth of the city followed as did the need for an expanded fire service.

This two-story, brick, Romanesque firehouse opened in 1899 as the department's first official station but was numbered as Fire Station No. 7 for Houston's paid fire service. The building features rusticated stone detailing, a five-bay front—one for a central arched entryway that is flanked by two apparatus bays. The station modified as it moved from horse-drawn carts to motorized vehicles, converting stables into stalls and adding accommodations for additional firefighters and equipment. It continued to be used as an active station until 1968, when Fire Station No. 7 was relocated. The building was restored in 1981, when it was converted into a museum, which it continues to serve as to this day.

ST. JAMES UNITED METHODIST CHURCH

1217 Wilson Street

Originally part of Trinity Methodist Episcopal Church, a small group of worshippers left in 1867 to organize a new Methodist congregation closer to their homes in Freedmen's Town. They began worshipping under a brush arbor along Buffalo Bayou before building a permanent structure in 1871. In 1908, upon learning that their church was within the newly defined borders of the city's red-light district, church members moved their building to the corner of Andrews and Wilson Streets in 1910.

Throughout the early part of the twentieth century, the church established how it was going to serve the community, forming programs for college-bound students, shut-ins, youth fellowship and a food ministry. This building, its newest sanctuary, was built in 1957 by African American architect J.J. Hawkins. The church served the parishioners under different names—West Point African Methodist Episcopal Church and Saint James Methodist Episcopal Church—before becoming the St. James United Methodist Church in 1968, following the merger of the Methodist and Evangelical United Brethren Churches.

THE SHERIDAN APARTMENTS

2603 Milam Streeet

A mixture of Art Deco and Spanish design, the Sheridan Apartments were constructed in 1922. The three-story apartment building was constructed to help ease a housing shortage in a rapidly expanding city. It is one of Houston's few remaining flats from that era and was listed as a Recorded Texas Historic Landmark in 1984. It was constructed on the

Constructed in 1922 to aid in a housing shortage in Houston, the Sheridan apartments are one of the few remaining flats from the 1920s and 1930s. They were built and owned by prominent railroad man and banker Robert C. Duff. *Author's collection.*

site of Houston's original baseball field, Herald Park, which was home to the Nationals, Heralds and Buffaloes (a.k.a. Houston Lambs and Houston Babies) from 1884 to 1904.

SEARS BUILDING

4201 Main Street

This four-story building was constructed in 1939, and the stand-alone Sears flagship department store was a landmark for nearly seventy-five years before finally closing its doors in January 2018. By the 1960s, its Art Deco design was considered outdated and old. Seeking a sleek new appearance, Sears shrouded the building in corrugated metal siding, a hip, modern and streamlined look at that time. However, the area was rife with unrest. With riots occurring or growing inflamed, the new paneling and bricked up windows also helped protect the building and its contents, just in case.

Recently, Rice University decided to take on the task of repurposing the shuttered building. It will become the Ion, a collaborative space for entrepreneurial, corporate and academic entities to come together with a mix of restaurant and entertainment offerings. The renovation will strip the building of its 1960s dress and will use signature elements of the original design. While many components will be retained, the building will not appear as the original 1939 structure.

UNIVERSITY OF ST. THOMAS

3800 Montrose Boulevard

This Catholic university was founded in 1947 and is the only one to serve the Archdiocese of Galveston-Houston. Classes began in the fall of 1947, with the first graduating class in 1951. The university was originally just the Link-Lee House, but it has expanded over the past sixty years with plans to cover twenty-five city blocks. It includes the starkly contrasting Chapel of St. Basil, which has dominated the campus since 1997. Many of the university's offices are in houses that were built in the 1930s scattered throughout campus.

RUTHERFORD B.H. YATES HOME

1314 Andrews Street

Home to Rutherford B.H. Yates Museum, the house is representative of the life, history and culture of Houston's Fourth Ward. The organization was formed in 1996 to save the house, and others in the Fourth Ward, from demolition, with the goal of restoring them and showcasing the history and lives of the freedmen who became doctors, lawyers, dentists, teachers, blacksmiths and inventors in Houston.

HUGHES HOUSE

3921 Yoakum

The theology department of St. Thomas is located in the childhood home of Howard Hughes. Built in 1918 and located on the south end of campus, this is where future businessman, film tycoon and aviator Howard Hughes spent his teenage years. He kept ownership of the home when he moved to California in 1925 so that his aunt could continue to live there. The university purchased the home in 1952 and originally used it for its social science building.

MUSEUM OF FINE ARTS, HOUSTON

1001 Bissonnet Street

Houston's Museum of Fine Arts (MFAH) is one of the largest museums in the United States and is the oldest art museum in Texas. Holding a permanent collection spanning more than six thousand years, there are approximately sixty-four thousand works from six continents. The site was dedicated in 1917 by the Houston Public School Art League, and its first museum building, the Watkin Building, opened in 1924.

Today, the MFAH is housed in two buildings, the Audrey Jones Beck Building, which opened in 2000, and the Caroline Wiess Law Building. The latter opened in 1926, with east and west wings added later in 1926 and subsequent additions in 1953, 1958 and 1974. Also, on the main campus

Located in the Freedmen's Town neighborhood, the Rutherford B.H. Yates Home has been converted into a museum dedicated to preserving the history of the family and African American printing. A handful of other nearby homes are slated for the same preservation and rehabilitation process. *Author's collection.*

The original Museum of Fine Arts, Houston, building was the first art museum to be built in Texas and was only the third in the South. Houston architect William Ward Watkin designed it for use as an art exhibition space, and it opened in 1924, with expansions starting as early as 1926. *Courtesy of Archives at the Museum of Fine Arts, Houston.*

are the Nancy and Rich Kinder Building, the Lillie and Hugh Roy Cullen Sculpture Garden, Glassell School of Art and a central administration building that includes the Glassell Junior School of Art. Off campus holdings include Bayou Bend Collection and Gardens, Rienzi and the Nidhika and Pershant Mehta Arts of India Gallery.

5

FIFTH WARD

As the city grew and population in the wards began to topple into disparity, the city decided to alter the ward districts. In December 1866, city leaders created the Fifth Ward, with two aldermen elected from that area. Buffalo Bayou served as the ward's southern border, while White Oak Bayou sat to the west. The city continued to draw the boundaries using natural landmarks and boundaries rather than using population density as a means of division.

Carved out of two other wards, the First and the Second, the original area was home to many Irish and Jewish settlers, the latter of which had fled Russia and eastern Europe. The area was prosperous. Following the Civil War, freed slaves began settling in the area, which was still sparsely populated. By the mid-1880s, the area was home to working-class people who plied their trade in the ship channel, industrial areas or as domestic help for wealthier Houstonians. Over the years, it became home to the city's minority and immigrant population with additional waves of Irish, German and Italian settlers.

The area almost seceded from the city but remained when its calls for improved municipal services were finally addressed. On February 21, 1912, the ward was almost destroyed. The Great Fifth Ward Fire began overnight in the rail yards, with strong winds spreading embers to wood-shingled roofs. In the end, the fire consumed a school, a church, thirteen industrial plants, eight stores and 119 homes. While there were no deaths, the fire caused more than $3 million in damages. In 1922, a group of Louisiana Creoles organized the community of Frenchtown, which saw an influx of settlers following the Great Mississippi Flood of 1927.

The cruiser USS *Houston* in the Ship Channel in 1930. Nearly 250,000 people visited the ship during its week-long visit. *Courtesy of National Archives.*

The ward prospered in the early twentieth century but began to slip after Interstate 10 was built through the Fifth Ward, dividing the community. Desegregation led to population loss, which resulted in subsequent commercial operations closing and the deterioration of homes and other buildings. Many of those remaining in the ward have lived there for generations. However, the area has yet to see some of the prosperity that other former wards have experienced, and it continues to struggle.

May 19, 1912, was the night of the costliest downtown fire. The fire began on the third floor of the six-story Stowers Furniture Building on Main Street. When it was extinguished, it had caused more than $1 million in damage. *Courtesy of Library of Congress.*

SCIENTIFIC BARBERSHOP

4610 Market Street

Willia Glenn Scott, better known as Bill, established the Scientific Barbershop around 1944. Ms. Scott had been trained at a barber college to learn the "science" of barbering. She lent that knowledge to her new business's name and becoming one of the few women barbers of the time. The barbershop quickly became a Fifth Ward institution—a gathering place for everyone from residents to politicians to exchange information and debate issues. Bill's sister Nannie Glenn went on to teach at Tyler Barber College in Houston, which trained most of the African American barbers in the state during the 1930s and 1940s. The two-story wood frame barbershop was built in 1949 and remains in the family.

SAINT ARNOLD BREWING COMPANY BUILDING

2000 Lyons Street

Saint Arnold Brewing Company is Texas's oldest craft brewery. It shipped its first keg of beer on June 9, 1994. Today, operations include the brewery, an on-site beer garden and restaurant, event space and guided tours of the facilities. The area northwest of the brewery was the location of the Great Fifth Ward Fire. Started in an abandoned building by transients attempting to keep warm, strong winds spread the fire as embers set wood-shingled roofs of the adjacent railyards on fire. This three-story brick building was constructed two years later for Houston Independent School District as a food service facility. Saint Arnold Brewing purchased it and repurposed it in 2009.

WHEATLEY HIGH SCHOOL

3415 Lyons Avenue

When Wheatley High School first opened in January 1927, it held classes here, in the old McGowan Elementary School building. It quickly became one of the largest black high schools in the nation and remained so throughout segregation. At its height, the music program drew in Duke Ellington to see musicians Archie Bell and Arnett Cobb, and the annual football game between Wheatley and Yates High Schools typically drew thirty thousand fans every Thanksgiving. By 1949, the facility was so overcrowded that students were forced to attend classes in shifts. Later that year, a new modernist campus—the most expensive high school in Houston at the time—located on Market Street opened and featured a large auditorium, gymnasium, industrial arts facility and swimming pool. Alumni include heavyweight champion George Foreman and Congresswoman Barbara Jordan.

6

SIXTH WARD

Within a decade of adding the Fifth Ward, Houston had grown enough to warrant the addition of another ward. In 1876, the Sixth Ward was carved out from the Fourth. The new political division, which began operating in 1877, used Buffalo Bayou to the south, Washington Avenue to the north and Glenwood Cemetery to the west as its boundaries to the city limits. It is the only ward that does not extend into downtown's historical center.

Originally, this land was part of a two-league Mexican land grant issued to John Austin in 1824 and was purchased by the Allen brothers in 1836 to establish the city. Much of the land was surveyed and sold off between 1839 and 1858. That same year, a good portion of the area was replatted into a lot and block system that is still evident in the Sixth Ward's layout today. Construction of homes on these lots began in 1860 and took off about a decade later when Washington Avenue was regraded.

Today, it is home to the oldest intact neighborhood in Houston, known as the Old Sixth Ward. Outside of Galveston, this area contains the largest concentration of Victorian homes in the region, with hundreds of homes dating between 1854 and 1935. In 1978, the neighborhood was listed on the National Register of Historic Places—the first in Houston to claim that notoriety.

Established in the late 1860s, an area called Vinegar Hill was located at the eastern terminus of Washington Avenue. It was considered a slum and was filled with one- and two-room box-shaped tenement houses. It was an early red-light and entertainment district and was considered unsafe and unlawful. Tin Can Alley, the main road that divided Vinegar Hill into two sections, was just as legendary as the area it was located within. By 1994, Vinegar Hill was demolished.

GLENWOOD CEMETERY

2525 Washington Avenue

Developed as a private cemetery in 1871, on the north side of Buffalo Bayou and west of downtown, in what was then the rural outskirts of Houston, Glenwood Cemetery's design is based on other nineteenth-century rural cemetery parks. It was the city's first professionally designed cemetery and was landscaped similar to parklands—filled with trees, long pathways along the uniquely rolling land of the bayou and wandering roads to travel. In addition to new private burials, many remains from the condemned St. Vincent's and Episcopal Cemeteries were reinterred here. Its parklike design drew visitors from throughout Houston, spurring the development of a mule-drawn trolley to get to Glenwood.

Developed in 1871, Glenwood Cemetery is the resting place of numerous influential Houstonians, including famed aviator and industrialist Howard Hughes and his parents. *Theo Smith.*

Today, the cemetery covers eighty-four acres (just large enough to drown out most of the modern noise) and has merged with the adjacent Washington Cemetery. Numerous historic markers pepper the grounds of Glenwood Cemetery and include the last president of the Republic of Texas, four governors, more than twenty Houston mayors, founders of oil companies, local religious and professional city leaders, eccentric billionaire Howard Hughes and his family and actress Gene Tierney.

WASHINGTON CEMETERY

2911 Washington Avenue

Established by the *Deutsche Gesellschaft von Houston* in 1887, the German Society Cemetery opened to the public for sales of family and single lots in 1887. When the United States entered the Great War, the anti-German rhetoric of the time led to the property being renamed Washington Cemetery. By this time, burials included immigrants from at least seventeen countries, with gravestones carved in English, German, French and Polish. From 1977 to 1999, the cemetery was restored, operated and maintained by a group of volunteers and, later, a trust before finally merging with the adjacent Glenwood Cemetery in 1999. A road connecting the two cemeteries was constructed in 2000, and to this day, Washington Cemetery remains an active cemetery.

HEIGHTS STATE BANK BUILDING

3620 Washington Avenue

This 1925 Neoclassical bank building has a more storied history as a live music venue than it does as a bank. In 1978, the building was rehabilitated into Rockefeller Hall, a nightclub hosting both local talent and established acts. The bank's small scale presented a unique performance space—the bank vault became an artist dressing room and the large lobby provided great acoustics. Rockefeller Hall served music fans for nearly two decades before shuttering. It served as an event venue before becoming a concert venue again in 2016. While many storied acts played here, it's rumored that Stevie Ray Vaughan's "The House is Rockin'" is about an evening at the Rockefeller.

Completed in 1925 for Heights State Bank, this building has a more storied history as Rockefeller Hall. In 1978, the building was transformed into an event venue. *Author's collection.*

FIRE STATION NO. 6

1702 Washington Avenue

Constructed in 1903, Fire Station No. 6 was one of the earliest stations to be built for Houston's paid fire service. The crew started out as Mechanic No. 6, organized as a volunteer company in 1873 and was located at the intersection of Washington Avenue and Preston Street, on what is today Bagby Street. Once the city established the paid city fire service, Station No. 6 received a new brick building, located at Washington Avenue and Ash Place. It has since been moved to stations at Henderson and Decatur (1931) and Washington and Lakin (1987).

After it was abandoned as a fire station in 1931, it served as an auction house and a salvage company before falling into disuse. In 2010, the building found a new owner who wanted to preserve the building and convert it into office space for his marketing firm. Construction began in 2010, and work preserved as much of the original structure as possible. It includes reclaimed bricks from another century-old building to be used in an expansion that would match the originals.

RIVIANA FOODS COMPLEX

1520 Sawyer Street

Marked with the logo of Mahatma Rice, the Riviana Foods complex was a mainstay in Houston's for eight decades—an obvious marker of the region's history of rice farming. With a new facility in Memphis, production and packaging at the Houston plant began phasing out in 2008, leaving only its headquarters offices behind (at a different location). Left behind in the Washington Avenue Arts District were warehouse spaces totaling seventy thousand square feet and an attached building housing nearly forty eighty-three-foot-high silos. Today, it's a complex of art studios, galleries and retail and restaurant space covering eight city blocks with a plan to expand more that includes Winter Street Studios, Spring Street Studios and the Shops at Sawyer Yards.

BUFFALO BAYOU PARK CISTERN

105 Sabine Street

Built in 1926, this was the location of Houston's first underground reservoir. Covering 87,500 square feet, 221 concrete pillars reach 25 feet to an eight-inch-thick concrete roof. Serving the city for decades as a drinking water reservoir, an irreparable leak eventually worked its way into the structure, causing the city to drain it and shut it down in 2007. While initially preparing to demolish it, plans for parking or storage were considered before forming a partnership with those developing Buffalo Bayou Park, which was right above them. The park added an entrance tunnel, railed walkway and some lighting and opened it to the public as both a history tour and an art installation.

PART III
OUTSIDE THE WARDS

1
THE HEIGHTS

Houston Heights, more commonly known as the Heights, began in the late nineteenth century as a budding suburb four miles outside of downtown Houston and only one and a half miles from Houston's Grand Central Depot. Built along White Oak Bayou and located along the Missouri, Kansas, Texas railroad line, it was named for its site on the high land (in comparison to the rest of the city) outside of Houston.

Around 1891, millionaire Oscar Martin Carter and a group of investors established the Omaha and South Texas Land Company, subdividing the site into residential and industrial districts as one of the first planned communities in Texas—Houston Heights. The company, under the direction of Treasurer Daniel Denton Cooley, began establishing the infrastructure of a new community—an electric rail system, parks, schools, streets, alleys and utilities. Other than commuting downtown for work, residents wouldn't have a reason to leave.

The city incorporated in 1893. The Heights added the Forest Park amusement center, an opera house, the Texas Christian Sanitarium, two newspapers, its own post office, a brick and tile manufacturer, a pickle factory and a sawmill. Larger homes began to rise, a high school opened in 1904 and two African American schools were operating by 1910. The city's population grew from 830 in 1900 to 6,000 just eight years later and again to 9,000 by 1915.

As the city of Houston encroached on the suburb's limits, residents finally voted for annexation in 1918. The area was starting to decline by the 1950s as suburbs with more and newer amenities sprouted up around Houston.

In 1973, the Houston Heights Association formed to preserve the city's first suburb, acquiring historic markers and achieving placement of more than one hundred structures on the National Register of Historic Places.

MORTON BROTHERS GROCERY

401 West Ninth Street

While common in early twentieth century neighborhoods, nonresidential commercial structures breaking up rows of homes are no longer the norm. The Heights features only a few remaining commercial structures. Built in 1928, Curtiss and William Morton operated their Morton Brothers Grocery until 1949, and it became a landmark location in the process. This one-story brick veneer commercial building was converted for use as a home in 1988, although remnants of its former life remain—large glass windows dominate the front, broken up by recessed double wooden doors in the center of the building.

HEIGHTS THEATER

339 West Nineteenth Street

Construction work began on a new theater in the Heights's downtown in 1928 and opened the following year. The Mission Revival–style movie house quickly became a center of activity in the community. The façade was modernized in 1935 to give it an Art Deco appearance, which it remains to this day. In 1968, the theater was damaged due to arson and sat empty for nearly two decades. It underwent a couple of rehabilitation projects in 1988 and again in 2015. It has been repurposed as a special event and concert venue. Visitors over the years have included Dan Rather, Gene Autry and even Bonnie and Clyde.

Originally built in a Mission Revival style, the Heights Theater was modernized in the Streamline Moderne style you see now. After the theater closed, it served as retail space before becoming a special event venue. *Author's collection.*

HOUSTON HEIGHTS FIRE STATION AND CITY HALL

107 West Twelfth Street

Little about this multiuse building has changed since it was completed in 1915. Designed as a combination city hall, jailhouse and fire station, the building housed five full-time firefighters, city council chambers, the judge's chambers, offices and a jail cell. It became Station No. 14 for the City of Houston Fire Department after annexation and was added to the National Register of Historic Places in 1983. It continued to be used for another seven decades, when it was finally replaced with a more updated facility.

Houston Heights Association refurbished the building, eventually purchasing it, adding a catering kitchen and chair lift and repairing the original tin ceiling in the process. Lockers belonging to the firefighters and one or two original fire poles remain. Bricks uncovered from the floor of the stables housing the horses that pulled fire equipment were relocated to one of the courtyards.

This two-story building was constructed as the home to Houston Heights' fire station, city hall and jail. After Houston Heights was annexed, it served as Fire Station No. 14 for the city of Houston from 1918 until 1995. *Author's collection.*

HOUSTON PUBLIC LIBRARY–HEIGHTS BRANCH

1302 Heights Boulevard

One of the first two branch libraries in Houston, the Heights branch opened in 1926. Originally located at Baptist Temple Church and then Heights High School, over the next fifty years, the library became a central gathering place for civic events, which resulted in the addition of a reading garden in 1939.

The library grew as the community did; a second-floor addition was added in 1951, air conditioning came in 1957 and the building was modernized during a 1979 rehabilitation. This last project increased the square footage slightly, replaced the reading garden with a community meeting center and addressed much-needed repairs but preserved the exterior historical integrity of the building while complementing any modern additions with the original.

HEIGHTS CHRISTIAN CHURCH

1703 Heights Boulevard

Constructed in 1927 as the permanent sanctuary for Heights Christian Church, this building was in continuous use for the next four decades. The congregation decided to move to a new building next door but retained ownership of this structure, using it for community events as Lambert Hall, named after the church's original pastor. Lambert Hall once served as home to the Heights Museum and has since housed Opera in the Heights, which worked with the congregation to renovate the building beginning in 1996, and Upstage Theatre.

HEIGHTS BOULEVARD ESPLANADE

The Heights Boulevard Esplanade was the first street constructed in the Heights and continues to be the main street running through the Heights. The pathway through Houston's first streetcar suburb is still lined with several early twentieth-century homes. Traveling along this magnolia- and palm-shaded thoroughfare, you'll discover architecture styles such as Queen Anne, Colonial and Craftsman built from pattern books. The one-and-a-half-mile-long median, or esplanade, is a wide landscaped park space containing pathways, a playground, gazebos, a Victorian rose garden and a World War II memorial.

HOUSTON HEIGHTS WATERWORKS RESERVOIR

West Twentieth and Nicolson Streets

The waterworks property has a 1928 concrete and brick reservoir building, a pumping station dating to 1939 and a pump building built in 1949. In 2017, plans called for the complex to be redeveloped into a collection of retail businesses and restaurants while maintaining its historical appearance.

HOUSTON HEIGHTS WOMAN'S CLUB

1846 Harvard Street

Daniel D. Cooley, who managed the Omaha and South Texas Land Company, built the Heights into the community it would become and owned numerous lots in the city. When his wife's birthday or their anniversary came around, he often transferred the land to her as presents. She donated one of those lots to the Houston Heights Woman's Club. The club had combined several earlier ladies' clubs that focused on arts, crafts, music and literary pursuits. With land in hand, the members raised $1,500 to construct their new home.

ORIENTAL TEXTILE MILL

2201 Lawrence Street

This complex of brick, mostly two-story industrial buildings is landmarked by a four-story clock tower. As a new residential and industrial community, the Heights boasted that it had the provisions to keep the two activities separated, making it attractive to industries. As one of the earliest industrial structures built in the Heights, it was joined by several manufacturing plants, oil refineries and mills in the formative years of the suburb. Best known as the Oriental Textile Mill, the complex was constructed in 1893 for a mattress manufacturing company. Over the years, the site has gone through several transformations as a textile mill, fiberglass manufacturer, bakery, Venetian blinds plant, mixed-use small business and living and working spaces.

JOHN MILROY HOUSE

1102 Heights Boulevard

Queen Anne–style Victorian homes are a fairly common sight in the Heights. The Milroy House, with its accompanying carriage house, was built in 1896 by developer Henry F. McGregor from designs published in pattern books that he slightly customized.

John Milroy was one of the officials associated with city founders Omaha and South Texas Land Company and served as an active civic leader, becoming an alderman and mayor of Houston Heights. This home was one of several dozen in the Heights built from his design and adapted by local builders. The Mansfield House, located at 1802 Harvard, was constructed in a similar fashion and remains one of the few original grand homes lining Heights Boulevard.

BANTA HOUSE

119 East Twentieth Street

A massive brick-and-concrete home built in 1918 is like no others in the area. While constructed in a Craftsman style, the Banta House's concrete columns and wraparound porches set it apart from its neighbors, giving it an iconic and steadfast appearance. The home, listed on the National Register of Historic Places in 1983, has most recently been used as office space for a mortgage and insurance company.

BARKER HOUSE

121 East Sixteenth Street

The one-time home of David Barker, who went on to serve as mayor of Houston Heights for six years, is a Colonial Revival, two-story frame house. The attached two-story porch wraps to one side and is supported by Doric columns, and the second-story porch is uncovered. Mayor Barker was active in the Heights's real estate, as well as civic and social activities in the community. The home retains a large corner lot and a modern patio addition.

THE CASTLE HOUSE

1802 Harvard Street

Considered to be the most iconic home in the Heights, this sprawling estate is lined with crepe myrtle trees and boasts five bedrooms, a carriage house and a guest house. It was one of many homes constructed by the original developers in 1892 and is one of only two remaining original homes, the other being the Milroy House.

The home has been meticulously preserved, featuring electric lights that date back to its building date, three baths, a sitting room, parlor, music room, sun porch, pool the original millwork and woodwork and more. Updates are rare, limited primarily to the addition or air conditioning. The house also features an aviary and koi pond.

DOUG'S BARBER SHOP

219 East Eleventh Street

An institution in the Heights since 1929, Doug's would be a throwback to the barbershops of yesteryear if it weren't where it has been for nearly a century. The shop still features a barber pole, steam towel straight razor shaves, tapered haircuts, shoeshines and low prices. Plastering the wall are items you might find in a history museum: vintage newspapers, old telephones, cash registers, model airplanes and numerous photographs.

Nearly every spot on the walls, and some parts of the ceiling, are filled with memorabilia. The shop is such an institution that when Houstonian Wes Anderson was scouting locations for his movie *Rushmore*, Doug's was one of the many locales chosen. If you decide to get a haircut, it's walk-in only, and make sure you are carrying cash.

2

RICE VILLAGE

Rice Village is one of Houston's oldest shopping destinations, as it opened in 1938. Located only a half mile from the center of Rice University, the central village covers several city blocks and is an amalgamation of old and new retail, restaurants, bars and more. During the 1950s and '60s, Rice Village boomed, filling nearly every space it could and causing a hodgepodge of unplanned development with homes and retail side by side. A bit of a bust hit the area in the 1970s, with development focused in more enclosed suburban shopping malls. A recent influx of newer, younger families and longtime residents in the neighborhoods surrounding Rice University and the Village have led to a revitalization in recent years. Today, Rice Village covers six blocks and is home to more than three hundred shops.

RICE UNIVERSITY

6100 Main Street

Chartered in May 1891 by Massachusetts-born businessman William Marsh Rice, the university was his gift to the city of Houston, the place where he made his fortune. Terms of the charter called for work on the educational institution to begin only after its benefactor's death. That date

Rice Village, located near Rice University's campus, is a collection of shops, restaurants and pubs. It is one of Houston's oldest shopping destinations and opened in 1938. *Author's collection.*

came unexpectedly on September 23, 1900. Charlie Jones, Rice's valet, conspired with lawyer Albert Patrick to murder Rice and claim his estate with a forged will. Following his autopsy, it was discovered that Jones had poisoned Rice with chloroform. Jones garnered immunity for his testimony. Patrick was sent to Sing Sing Correctional Facility for murder, only to be pardoned (on the anniversary day of Rice's murder) in 1912, the same year that classes began at the William Marsh Rice Institute for the Advancement of Literature, Science and Art—better known then as Rice Institute.

Today, Rice is a research university with an undergraduate focus. It is nationally recognized and noted for its programs in applied sciences, such as artificial heart research and nanotechnology. The university is organized into eleven residential colleges and eight schools, competes in fourteen NCAA Division I varsity sports and is part of Conference USA. Prominent alumni include astronauts, space scientists, CEOs and founders of Fortune 500 companies, members of Congress, presidential cabinet secretaries, judges, mayors, two Nobel Prize winners, two Pulitzer Prize winners and numerous Fulbright scholars, Marshall scholars, Mellon fellows and Rhodes scholars.

Rice University opened in 1912 following the murder of its namesake William Marsh Rice. Today, it is a private research university with an undergraduate focus and is one of the toughest schools to gain admission to, rivaling many Ivy League schools. *Author's collection.*

In 2011, *Travel + Leisure* listed Rice as one of the most beautiful campuses in the United States. The university's first president, Edgar Odell Lovett, wanted the campus to be uniform in style. Therefore, nearly all campus buildings are Byzantine in style, with sand and pink bricks, and feature large archways and columns. The following are a few of the most notable buildings on campus.

LOVETT HALL

Named for the first president of Rice, this is likely the most iconic building on campus and is also known as the administration building. Featuring a sally port arch, it serves as a symbol for students entering during matriculation and departing as graduates. Upon closer inspection, the architectural detail on the hall's columns alone is a highlight and could keep one busy for hours. This was the first building on campus and today houses the admission office and welcome center.

Mechanical Laboratory and Central Plant

Formerly known as the Power House, this was the second building constructed on campus. Until South Plant was built about a century later, this complex served as the campus's only power plant, and it still provides power to much of the campus. Hiding its smokestack is a 140-foot-tall campanile.

Baker College—Commons

Formerly called the Central Dining Hall, this was one of the four original buildings on campus, all designed and constructed by the Cram, Goodhue and Ferguson firm out of Boston. For forty-three years, this building, featuring high-vaulted ceilings and engraved oak beams, served as the lone campus dining hall. Today, it serves as a common meeting space and dining area.

Wiess President's House

This home, constructed in 1920 on the corner of Sunset and Main, was originally the home to Harry Carothers Wiess and his family. It was donated by the family to Rice University in 1974. It was leased following the donation and then sat empty beginning in 1990. It has since been renovated and now serves as the Rice University president's residence.

Rice Stadium

6100 South Main Street

Rice Stadium has been home to the Rice Owls football team since it was completed in 1950 and replaced Rice Field. It is an example of modern architecture: simple, functional and unadorned. It was built solely for football, and, partly because of its sightlines to the field, it is considered one of the best stadiums in the state for watching a game.

Entrances and aisles were designed so the stadium could be emptied in nine minutes. In 2015, the Brian Patterson Sports Performance Center took over a generally unused portion of the north end of the stadium and provides training and office amenities for the Owls football team.

Rice Stadium has been the home of the Rice Owls football team since its completion in 1950. It also served as the host of Super Bowl VIII between the Minnesota Vikings and Miami Dolphins. *Author's collection.*

Over the years, Rice Stadium also served as the home to University of Houston football (1951–65) and the Houston Oilers (1965–67) and hosted the Bluebonnet Bowl (1959–1967, 1985–1986), Super Bowl VIII (1974) and numerous concerts. On September 12, 1962, it was the site of President John F. Kennedy's "we choose to go to the moon" speech, which challenged Americans to send a man to the moon by the end of the decade.

TUDOR FIELDHOUSE

Previously known as Rice Gymnasium (1950–2008), the Tudor Fieldhouse serves as a multipurpose arena on campus. The court is designated as Autry Court in memory of Mrs. James L. Autry, whose daughter made a generous donation during its construction. It is home to the Owl's basketball and volleyball teams and, previously, swim teams. In 1991, renovations brought a new ceiling, new lighting, a new scoreboard and air conditioning. Additional renovations came in 2007, and it was renamed Tudor Fieldhouse. During construction fourteen home games were split between Merrell Center, Reliant Arena and Toyota Center.

3

RIVER OAKS

River Oaks, Houston's first residential garden suburb, was created in the 1920s by attorney Hugh Potter and brothers William and Michael Hogg, sons of former Texas governor Jim Hogg. The group retained famed Kansas City landscape architects Hare and Hare to provide a master plan that would protect the surrounding natural environment of the area and J.C. Nichols, also of Kansas City, to serve as the community's design consultant.

The plan included a variety of homesites, a fifteen-acre campus for River Oaks Elementary School, two shopping centers and esplanades planted with flowers. All utility lines were to be hidden underground, there were to be no alleyways, only three intersecting streets were allowed and all commercial traffic was banned. To remain exclusive, deed restrictions and required architect-approved house designs were enacted. A minimum purchase price was also established, as was a "gentlemen's agreement," which meant that there was an understanding that the community excluded blacks, Jews and other minorities from living in River Oaks.

As the community coalesced, River Oaks became a well-publicized national model for its community planning. Homes, while unique in layout, had a distinct appearance. Those along Kirby, for example, were restricted to American Colonial or English Tudor style. While the community development lost money as it grew throughout the 1920s, and while it operated independently for its first three years, it was eventually annexed by the City of Houston. By the late 1930s, it was the opposite.

Developers had invested $3 million in the project, and River Oaks' development began to influence how patterns played out downtown. By the 1990s, River Oaks was the geographic center of Houston. It is home to the River Oaks Country Club and in 2013 was named the most expensive neighborhood in Houston.

RIVER OAKS CORPORATION HOUSE

2164 Troon Road

This house was designed by Charles Oliver as a speculative house for the River Oaks Corporation. Built in 1929 and 1930, the Colonial Revival home is situated on a block of Troon Road that is one of the most architecturally intact areas in Houston's posh River Oaks neighborhood; three of the homes are listed as City of Houston Historic Landmarks. During construction only three other homeowners lived on Troon Street, with two other houses in the construction phase. When new homes were advertised in 1930, they were offered in three price ranges, and this one appeared in the highest of those levels. The brick veneer, two-story speculative home was purchased and occupied by 1932.

RIVER OAKS THEATRE

2009 West Gray Street

The Art Deco–style River Oaks Theatre opened in 1939. Ownership and operation changed hands several times in the next thirty years, until 1977, when it was under the control of Movie Inc. Its focus changed from first-run to alternative films, which included rereleased titles, classic and foreign films and cult movies, such as the *Rocky Horror Picture Show*, which was a mainstay for a number of years.

The theater returned to first-run films in the 1980s during the rise of VHS, rentals and cable television. This period also saw a massive renovation to the theater, including seating capacity, a new projector and sound system, the installation of a café upstairs and the alteration of its balcony into two 125-seat mini theaters. Today, the theater is an art house cinema.

Located in the River Oaks shopping center, this historic theater continues to operate under its intended purpose, although it has been slightly altered. It currently houses three projection screens: one large screen downstairs and two smaller screens upstairs in the space that used to be the balcony. *Author's collection.*

RIENZI

1406 Kirby Drive

The Rienzi is the Museum of Fine Arts' museum for European decorative arts. Situated on four acres of wooded gardens, this is the former home of philanthropists Carroll Sterling Masterson and Harris Masterson III. It was named for Rienzi Johnston, Mr. Masterson's grandfather and was designed in 1952 by Houston architect John Staub, who also designed Bayou Bend. Rienzi opened to the public in 1999 and houses a collection that includes paintings, furnishings, porcelain and miniatures.

RIVER OAKS SHOPPING CENTER

2009 West Gray Street

Considered the third-oldest shopping center of its type in the United States, the River Oaks Shopping Center opened to shoppers in November 1937. The center was an important part of the implementation for the River Oaks master planned community, providing convenience and commerce not only for River Oaks but also for the rest of Houston's residents. The center ran along both sides of West Gray Avenue, and the two main buildings were mirror images of one another. They had a semicircular shape, allowing automobile drivers entering the center to see all of the stores available to them. The architects wanted the shops to speak for themselves, giving the appearance of minimalist design and detail with large windows. Portions of the original center have been demolished, and concerns have continued about the future fate of the rest of the complex.

BAYOU BEND

1 Westcott Street

Located on fourteen acres of land along Buffalo Bayou, Bayou Bend was the estate of socialite Ima Hogg. The estate slopes to the north from its original entrance on Lazy Lane and winds down terraced lawn steps toward Diana Garden and the bayou. The two-story, twenty-four-room house and adjacent two-story garage and service building were constructed from 1926 to 1928 by John Staub for Ima and her two unmarried brothers, William and Michael, who were the developers of River Oaks. Modeled after early nineteenth-century English homes with details inspired by eighteenth- and nineteenth-century American South homes, the building is a tile block construction with an exterior pink stucco finish and a raised seam copper roof—a style that Ima Hogg called "Latin Colonial."

In 1920, Ima Hogg began a collection of seventeenth- through early nineteenth-century American furniture, paintings and artifacts that started with the purchase of an eighteenth-century American Queen Anne armchair. After her brother Mike's marriage in 1929 and Will's death the following year, Ima occupied the house alone, continuing to grow her collection until 1965. In 1956, Hogg donated the estate and its contents to the Museum of Fine Arts Houston, which began converting the home into a museum in the mid-1960s. The collection opened to the public as the Bayou Bend Collection in March 1966 and is now considered one of the finest assortments of American decorative arts and paintings spanning from the 1660s through the 1860s. The gardens are maintained by the River Oaks Garden Club, the property features a historical marker and is listed on the National Register of Historic Places.

ALABAMA THEATER

2922 South Shepherd Drive

Currently housing a Trader Joe's grocery store, the Alabama Theater has had a tumultuous past decade or so. The historic Art Deco/Streamline Moderne movie theater opened in 1939, catering to the Upper Kirby and River Oaks neighborhoods. The theater closed in the early 1980s and reopened as the Alabama Bookstop bookstore in 1984. The owners preserved the theater's murals and balconies, while attempting to protect as much of its architecture as possible during renovations. After being sold to Weingarten Realty in 2004, the bookstore closed in 2009, under threat of demolition. In 2011, Trader Joe's saved the historic theater by moving in with a renovation plan that would help preserve the building's integrity. It was the company's first Houston location.

The Alabama Theatre opened in 1939, screening Jack Benny's *Man About Town*. It has since served as a bookstore and is occupied by a Trader Joe's. While some modifications have been made to the property, it still maintains some of its historic appearance. *Courtesy of Library of Congress.*

LAMAR HIGH SCHOOL

3325 Westheimer Road

Lamar High School, named for Texas revolutionary leader and second president of the Republic of Texas Mirabeau B. Lamar, is within the Houston Independent School District. The school was built in 1936 on the former site of Michael Westheimer's farm. Westheimer was a German immigrant who arrived in Houston in 1859, purchasing a 640-acre farm where he established a school for local children. The path to the school, Westheimer's Road, is now one of the most recognizable street names in Houston.

When the high school opened, it was considered the equivalent of an exclusive prep school and was located on the southern end of the River Oaks Boulevard. The campus consists of four buildings, a baseball field, a football field and tennis courts. The original building is North Building, which is four stories tall (including the basement) and consists of classrooms, administrative offices, an auditorium, a band room, a cooking room and a choir room. The Art Deco building is constructed of Texas limestone, and the auditorium entryway is decorated with a relief map of Texas.

The school is used as the setting for Grover Cleveland High School in *Rushmore* and was featured in the Chuck Norris film *Sidekicks*. The list of notable alumni is long but includes former television journalist Linda Ellerbee, auto racing champion A.J. Foyt, actress Lisa Hartman-Black, singer Kelly Rowland, actress Jaclyn Smith and danceer/choreographer/actor Tommy Tune.

HERMANN PARK

6001 Fannin Street

This 445-acre urban park is bounded by Houston's museum district to the north, with Texas Medical Center and Brays Bayou to the west and sits just west and adjacent to the Third Ward. It is one of Houston's oldest public parks and is home to numerous landscaped features, such as a reflecting pool, gardens and the 8-acre McGovern Lake, as well as a number of cultural institutions and the first desegregated public golf course in the United States, Hermann Park Golf Course.

Right: This statue of General Sam Houston stands guard over Hermann Park. General Houston led early Texans to victory to obtain independence from Mexico in 1839. He helped establish the new Republic of Texas and served as its first president. *Courtesy of National Archives.*

Below: The Mecom Fountain, located in a traffic circle at Main and Montrose Streets, has been a beacon at the edge of the park since 1964. The fountain, designed by Eugene Werlin, was the largest in the city at the time of completion. *Author's collection.*

Following an urban planning effort by the city in 1913, George Hermann, who sat on the parks board, donated his estate to Houston for use as a public green space in 1914. Renowned landscape architect George Kessler created a master plan for the park in 1916, and over the next decade, it began to take shape. Through the years, the park grew and was altered before it was neglected and transformed. Today, it is one of the largest urban parks located in the city of Houston. It features the 1964 Mecom Fountain and the 1925 Sam Houston equestrian sculpture atop a granite arch. The city continues to improve the park for the needs of all Houstonians.

HOUSTON ZOO

6200 Hermann Park Drive

The fifty-five-acre Houston Zoo houses more than six thousand animals from five hundred species and is the second-most-visited zoo in the United States. While it has been run by a nonprofit since 2001, it was originally operated by the City of Houston. The first resident of the Houston Zoo was a bison named Earl who was donated from a traveling circus. The original zoo was located at Sam Houston Park, in downtown Houston. In addition to Earl, the growing collection briefly included the retired horses of the Houston Fire Department. Today, the zoo creates unique habitats designed and stylized for the animal's behavioral and native needs.

MILLER OUTDOOR THEATER

6000 Hermann Park Drive

This outdoor theater opened to the public in 1923. Built as an amphitheater-style hillside, the theater was designed to be surrounded by twenty Corinthian-style limestone columns. The adjacent seating, Miller's Hill, was created in 1948, and in 1968, the city built a new theater. That new building was refurbished in 1996.

This aerial shot of the Hermann Park entrance showcases one of Houston's finest outdoor recreational centers. It is one of Houston's oldest public parks and was designed by famed landscape architect George Kessler. *Courtesy of National Archives.*

HOUSTON MUSEUM OF NATURAL SCIENCE

5555 Hermann Park Drive

Established by the Houston Museum and Scientific Society in 1909, the original goal of the museum was to provide a free institution that focused on education and science. Today, the complex consists of a central museum with four floors of exhibits, a planetarium, a theater and the Cockrell Butterfly Center. Much of the original collection came through acquisitions between 1914 and 1930. It was originally housed in Houston's city auditorium, then the Central Library and, in 1929, a site located within the Houston Zoo. Renamed the Houston Museum of Natural Science in 1960, it moved into a structure built for the museum in 1969.

4

OTHER NOTABLE LANDMARKS

SAN JACINTO BATTLEGROUND STATE HISTORIC SITE

3523 Independence Parkway

Located on the Ship Channel, the San Jacinto Monument is the centerpiece of this state historic site. Standing as the world's tallest masonry column and topped with a 220-ton star, this site commemorates the site of the Battle of San Jacinto, the decisive battle of the Texas Revolution. The monument opened in 1939 and features an observation deck at the top, the San Jacinto Museum of History in its base and markers dotting the landscape below, outlining the movement and action during the April 1836 battle. Under General Sam Houston's Army of Texas, the Mexican army of General Santa Anna was defeated, bringing the cry "Remember the Alamo" to prominence and providing Texas its freedom.

MOODY PARK

3725 Fulton Street

Moody Park opened in 1925 in Near Northside. Named for politician Alvin S. Moody, the park features a small gymnasium, meeting rooms, a public swimming pool, baseball fields, Luis A. Jiminez's fiberglass installation *The Vaquero* and a rail station.

(O-2679-535I-22SQ)(6-I3-39-IOAM)(I2") SAN JACINTO MONUMENT, HOUSTON, TEXAS

The San Jacinto Monument marks the spot of the Battle of San Jacinto, the decisive battle of the Texas Revolution. At 567.31 feet tall, it is the world's tallest masonry column. *Courtesy of National Archives.*

On May 7, 1978, it was the scene of the Moody Park riots, which stemmed from protests over the controversial killing of Jose Campos Torres while in police custody. The riots led to more than forty arrests, a dozen hospitalizations and hundreds of thousands of dollars of property damage. In the aftermath, while relations between police and community were strained, it eventually led to police reforms.

MEMORIAL PARK

6501 Memorial Drive

Memorial Park opened in 1924 and now covers nearly 1,500 acres. It is one of the largest urban parks in the country. Originally designed by Kansas City landscape architects Hare and Hare, this area was formerly Camp Logan, a United States Army training encampment, which was much larger than the park is today. In 1924, Will and Mike Hogg purchased 1,500 acres of the campsite and sold it to the city at cost. The city converted it into a memorial park dedicated to fallen World War I soldiers.

At Camp Logan on the night of August 23, 1917, African American soldiers rioted against the City of Houston. The Twenty-Fourth United States Infantry Regiment, following repeated acts of racist language, actions and violence against them by members of the Houston Police Department, decided enough was enough. That night, a group of soldiers marched toward downtown. This resulted in the deaths of eleven civilians, five policemen and four soldiers. The rioting soldiers were tried at three courts-martial for mutiny, resulting in nineteen executions and forty-one life sentences.

Today, the park includes a golf course (fourteen-time host to the PGA Tour's Houston Open), facilities for multiple sports activities and the Houston Arboretum and Nature Center. Nearly twice the size of New York's Central Park, it continues to grow and transform to the needs of its visitors. There are currently plans for a land bridge and central connector that will help ease traffic and restore parkland at the same time.

Camp Logan, seen here in 1918, was a World War I–era army training camp. The site of the camp is primarily occupied by Memorial Park. Many of the park's trails trace old Camp Logan roads. African American soldiers from the camp led a riot in 1917 and saw more than six hundred cases reported during the 1918 flu pandemic. Only a few remnants of Camp Logan remain in the park. *Courtesy of National Archives.*

PORT OF HOUSTON

111 East Loop North

The Port of Houston is one of the world's largest ports, stretching twenty-five miles as a complex of public and private facilities. It is only a few hours sailing time from the Gulf of Mexico. It is the busiest port in the United States in terms of foreign tonnage, second busiest in terms of overall tonnage and sixteenth busiest in the world. The original port was downtown at the confluence of Buffalo and White Oak Bayous, now known as Allen's Landing. Over time, shipping points began to sprout up along Buffalo Bayou, at the Port of Harrisburg and the docks at Allen Ranch. By the end of the century, it had become a major shipping channel, rivaling Galveston. Following the destruction of the Galveston hurricane in 1900, Harris County voters approved plans to create a modern port in 1909, hoping an inland port would be better suited. It opened in 1914. Visitors wishing to experience the port and its activities can hitch a ride on a tour boat, but it remains a popular excursion and is sometimes booked months in advance.

Freighter leaving the Port of Houston, 1939. It is riding high because it has yet to load its cargo at Galveston. *Courtesy of Library of Congress.*

JOHNSON SPACE CENTER

2101 East NASA Parkway

The Johnson Space Center is home to NASA's Mission Control and astronaut training and research facilities. Originally called the Manned Spacecraft Center when it opened in 1961, it was renamed after Texas native and late president Lyndon B. Johnson in 1973. The center consists of a complex of one hundred buildings in the Clear Lake area and served as Mission Control for the *Gemini, Apollo, Skylab, Apollo-Soyuz* and all space shuttle program flights. It currently directs U.S. activities aboard the International Space Station. The Apollo Mission Control Center, a National Historic Landmark, is located in building 30.

Space Center Houston, the official visitor center of Johnson Space Center, hosts more than four hundred space artifacts, permanent and traveling exhibits (including space craft), attractions, live shows and more, all dedicated to the history of America's human spaceflight program.

Space Center Houston is the official visitor center of NASA's Johnson Space Center and is home to Mission Control and astronaut training. The center opened in 1992, preserving the story of Houston's role in space exploration since 1961. *Author's collection.*

Additional attractions include Independence Plaza, which contains the world's only space shuttle replica mounted on an original shuttle carrier aircraft; a NASA tram tour that includes building 30; and Rocket Park, which includes a restored Saturn V rocket.

ASTRODOME

8400 Kirby Drive

When the dome opened in 1965, it was officially known as the Harris County Domed Stadium and has been known since as the Houston Astrodome or the Eighth Wonder of the World. It was the world's first multipurpose, domed sports stadium and led to the invention of AstroTurf after the original grass died. It served as the home of the Houston Astros until 1999, the Houston Oilers from 1968 until 1996 and the Houston Rockets part-time from 1971 until 1975. It was also the primary venue of the Houston Livestock Show and

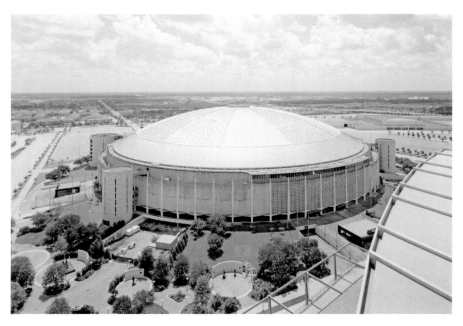

The Astrodome, nicknamed the Eighth Wonder of the World, is the world's first multipurpose, domed sports stadium. It has served as the home to MLB's Astros, NFL's Oilers and NBA's Rockets and was the primary venue for the Houston Livestock Show and Rodeo from 1966 until 2002. *Courtesy of Library of Congress.*

Rodeo from 1966 until 2002, having supplanted downtown's Sam Houston Coliseum and now replaced by the adjacent NRG Stadium. After several years of disuse, portions were demolished but interest has been renewed to repurpose the structure. It was listed on the National Register of Historic Places in 2014.

ELLINGTON FIELD/LONE STAR FLIGHT MUSEUM

11551 Aerospace Avenue

Ellington Field Joint Reserve Base is now a joint installation shared by various active and reserve military units as well as NASA. The base itself is limited to on-site visitors. However, the Lone Start Flight Museum is located adjacent to it and is open to the public. Ellington Field opened in 1917 as one of thirty-two air service training camps after the United States entered World War I. It had a variety of uses throughout much of the twentieth century, including astronaut flight proficiency training by NASA. While inactivated by the air force in 1976, the Texas Air National Guard, Texas Army National Guard, U.S. Coast Guard, Civil Air Patrol and the Reserves for the United States Army, navy and marines still maintain a presence on the base. The Lone Star Flight Museum relocated from Galveston to this location in 2017 and is an aviation museum and STEM learning center. It houses the Texas Aviation Hall of Fame, a large flying collection of historic aircraft and several exhibits.

BLUE TILE STREET MARKERS

Throughout Houston

Embedded in curbs throughout Houston, primarily in the neighborhoods surrounding downtown, are blue tile street markers that are used to denote street numbering and names and occasionally the name of a business. This form of street identification, blue lettering and numbering on a white tile background, started in the 1920s and continued into the early 1950s. It was cheap, durable and easy to read in the slower-moving cars of the day. As traffic picked up in number and speed, these street markers became more difficult to read and fell out of style. Today, many are in a state of deterioration or destruction, although a number of them can be found throughout the city. There are few left in downtown Houston, but they can be found more prominently in the neighborhoods surrounding downtown.

THE BEER CAN HOUSE

222 Malone Street

Retired Southern Pacific Railroad upholsterer John Milkovisch started a new project in 1968. Frustrated with ongoing yard work, Milkovisch began inlaying thousands of rocks, marbles and metal pieces into concrete and redwood around his yard, creating a unique landscape. When he finished his yard, he focused on his house. Using transformed beer cans (flattened, cut, shaped, etc.), he began siding his house, and over the next eighteen years, the house was covered—not just in siding but also with garlands, windchimes and decorative additions. More than fifty thousand cans were used in the process. Open to the public for viewing and tours, the house has become a folk art landmark in Houston.

BIBLIOGRAPHY

Books

Alexander, Drury Blakeley. *Texas Home of the Nineteenth Century*. Austin: University of Texas Press, 1966.

Andrews, Michael. *Historic Texas Courthouses*. Houston, TX: Bright Sky Press, 2006

Baker, Eugene C., ed. *History of Texas and Texans*. Vol. 3. Chicago: American Historical Society, 1914.

Carroll, B.H. *Standard History of Houston*. Knoxville, TN: H.W. Crew, 1912.

Chapman, Betty T. *Historic Houston: An Illustrated History and Resource Guide*. San Antonio, TX: Lamert Publications, 1997.

———. *100 Years—100 Stories: Houston Public Library 1904–2004*. Houston, TX: Houston Public Library, 2004.

Ching, Francis D.K. *A Visual Dictionary of Architecture*. New York: John Wiley and Sons, 1995.

Dressman, Fran. *Gus Wortham: Portrait of a Leader*. College Station: Texas A&M University Press, 1994.

Echols, Gordon. *Early Texas Architecture*. Fort Worth: Texas Christian University Press, 2000.

Farrar, R.M. *Buffalo Bayou and the Houston Ship Channel, 1820–1926*. Houston, TX: Chamber of Commerce, 1926.

Federal Writer's Program. *Houston: A History and Guide. American Guide Series*. Houston, TX: Anson Jones Press, 1942.

Fenberg, Steven. *Unprecedented Power: Jesse Jones, Capitalism, and the Common Good*. College Station: Texas A&M University Press, 2011.

Field, William Scott. *Last of the Past: Houston Architecture 1847–1915*. Houston, TX: Harris County Heritage Society, 1980.

Fox, Stephen. *Houston Architectural Guide*. Houston, TX: American Institute of Architects/Houston Chapter and Herring Press, 2012.

Goeldner, Paul. *Historic American Buildings Survey, Texas Catalog*. San Antonio, TX: Trinity University Press, 1993.

Green, Charles D. *Fire Fighters of Houston, 1836–1915*. Houston, TX: Charles D. Green, 1915.

Harris, Cyril. *Dictionary of Architecture and Construction*. New York: McGraw-Hill, 2006.

Hatch, Orin Walker. *Lyceum to Library: A Chapter in the Cultural History of Houston*. Houston: Texas Gulf Coast Historical Association, 1965.

Henry, Jay C. *Architecture in Texas: 1895–1945*. Austin: University of Texas Press, 1993.

Houghton, Dorothy Knox Howe, Barrie Scardino Bradley, and Katherine S. Howe. *Houston's Forgotten Heritage: Landscape, Houses, Interiors 1824–1914*. Houston, TX: Rice University Press, 1991.

James, Marquis. *The Texaco Story: The First Fifty Years, 1902–1952*. Houston: Texas Company, 1953.

Johnston, Marguerite. *Houston: The Unknown City, 1836–1946*. College Station: Texas A&M University Press, 1991.

Kelsey, Mavis Parrott, Sr., and Donald Dyal. *The Courthouses of Texas*. College Station: Texas A&M University Press, 2007.

Larson, Henrietta. *History of Humble Oil and Refining Company*. Hanover, NH: Ayer Publication, 1993.

Longstreth, Richard. *The Buildings of Main Street: A Guide to American Commercial Architecture*. Walnut Creek, CA: AltaMira, 2000.

McComb, David. *Houston: A History*. Austin: University of Texas Press, 1981.

Mod, Anna. *Building Modern Houston*. Charleston, SC: Arcadia Publishing, 2011.

Niemeyer, Daniel. *1950s American Style: A Reference Guide*. Boulder, CO: Fifties Book Publishers, 2013.

Parsons, Jim, and David Bush. *Houston Deco: Modernistic Architecture of the Texas Coast*. Houston, TX: Bright Sky Press, 2008.

Poppeliers, J.C. *What Style Is It? A Guide to American Architecture*. Washington, D.C.: Preservation Press, 1983.

Powell, William Dylan. *Lost Houston*. Chicago: Pavilion Books, 2016.

Scardin, Barrie, William F. Stern, and Bruce C. Webb. *Ephemeral City: Cite Looks at Houston*. Austin: University of Texas, 2003.

Sibley, Marilyn McAdams. *The Port of Houston: A History*. Austin: University of Texas Press, 1968.

Sigel, Stanley E. *Houston: A Chronicle of the Supercity on Buffalo Bayou*. Woodland Hills, CA: Windsor, 1983.

Smith, Tristan, and Fire Museum of Houston. *Houston Fire Department*. Charleston, SC: Arcadia Publishing, 2015.

Speck, Lawrence W. *Landmarks of Texas Architecture*. Austin: University of Texas Press, 2012.

Sterling, Ross. *Ross Sterling, Texan: A Memoir by the Founder of Humble Oil and Refining Company*. Austin: University of Texas Press, 2010.

Strom, Steven R. *Houston: Lost and Unbuilt*. Austin: University of Texas Press, 2010.

———. *Houston on the Move: A Photographic History*. Austin: University of Texas Press, 2016.

Thomas, Bernice L. *America's 5 & 10 Cent Stores: The Kress Legacy*. New York: John Wiley and Sons, 1997.

Tyler, Ron, Douglas Barnett, and Roy R. Barkley, eds. *The New Handbook of Texas*. Austin: Texas State Historical Association, 1996.

Welling, David. *Cinema Houston: From Nickelodeon to Cineplex*. Austin: University of Texas Press, 2007.

Whiffen, Marcus. *American Architecture Since 1780—A Guide to the Styles*. Cambridge, MA: MIT Press, 1969.

Withey, Henry F., and Elsie Rathburn. *Biographical Dictionary of American Architects: Deceased*. Los Angeles: Hennessey and Ingalls, 1970.

Young, Samuel Oliver. *A Thumbnail History of the City of Houston, Texas: 1836–1912*. Houston, TX: Rein and Son, 1912.

———. *True Stories of Old Houston and Houstonians*. Galveston, TX, O. Springer, 1913.

Publications

Blankenhorn, Dana. "James A. Elkins, Sr.: For Half a Century 'The Judge' Held Reigns of Houston Power." *Houston Business Journal*, September 24, 1984.

Bryant, Keith, L., Jr. "Railway Stations of Texas: A Disappearing Architectural Heritage." *Southwestern Historical Quarterly* 79, no. 4 (April 1976): 417–40.

Chapman, Betty T. "Story of Public Libraries Took Long Time to Write in Houston." *Houston Business Journal,* June 2, 2000.

Dodds, George. "Follow the Money: Houston's Third Federal Reserve Building." *Cite: The Architecture and Design Review of Houston* 65 (Winter 2005): 16–19.

Elliot, Margie C., and Charles D Maynard, Jr. "The Rice Hotel." *Cite: The Architecture and Design Review of Houston* 29 (Fall 1992–Winter 1993): 21–22.

Fox, Stephen. "Sanguinet and Staats in Houston, 1903–1926." *Perspective* 12, no. 1 (Spring 1983): 2–11.

———. "The Warehouse District: An Architectural Tour." *Cite: The Architecture and Design Review of Houston* 17 (Spring 1987): 14–15.

Hoffmeyer, Michael. "Public Buildings of Sanguinet and Staats." *Perspective* 10, no. 1 (Spring 1981): 23–27.

Koush, Ben. "The Modern Mr. Jones: A Legendary Houston Architect Shares His Tall Building Portfolio." *Cite: The Architecture and Design Review of Houston* 72 (Fall 2007): 30–35.

Ochsner, Jeffrey Karl. "Tall Buildings: Houston as a Case in Point." *Texas Architect* 32 (May/June 1982), 38–45.

Rogers, Karen Hess. "The Rice Hotel...Rice Institute Connection." *Cornerstone* 5, no. 1 (Fall 1999): 1–8.

Smith, Frank P. "A Detailed Description of the Port." *Houston Port Book* 13 (May 1935): 19–21.

Strom, Steven R. "Remembering Houston: Seeing the City through the Eyes of Bob Bailey." *Cite: The Architecture and Design Review of Houston* 67 (Summer 2006): 17–23.

Sturrock, Sidonie. "A Detective on the Case: Uncovering the Story of Quality Hill, Houston's First Elite Residential Neighborhood." *Houston History* 12, no. 2 (Spring 2015): 7–12.

Victor, Sally. "The Gulf Building, Houston, Texas." *Perspective* 13, no. 1 (1984): 2–8.

Wilson, Michael E. "Alfred C. Finn: Houston Architect." *Houston Review* 5, no. 2 (Summer 1983): 64–80.

Electronic Sources

Bivins, Ralph. "Tearing Down History: Houston's Shameful Disdain of Historic Preservation Must Stop." *Culture Map: Houston,* October 17, 2014. http://houston.culturemap.com.

City of Houston Planning and Development. "Main Street Market Square." *Historic Preservation Manual*, 2013. http://www.houstontx.gov.

Cook, Lynn. "Downtown's Sweeney, Combs Building Sells to Houston Group." *Houston Business Journal*, September 21, 1998. http://www.bizjournals.com.

DeBardelaben, Rebecca. "A Witness to History." *In the Belly of the Beast: A People's Guide to Houston* (blog), May 14, 2009. https://peoplesguidetohouston.wordpress.com.

Ferrer, Ada. "Democratic National Convention of 1928." *Handbook of Texas Online*. Texas State Historical Association, June 12, 2010. https://tshaonline.org.

Fox, Stephen. "Finger, Joseph." *Handbook of Texas Online*. Texas State Historical Association, June 12, 2010. https://tshaonline.org.

———. "Heiner, Eugene T." *Handbook of Texas Online*. Texas State Historical Association, June 15, 2010. https://tshaonline.org.

———. "Shelor Motor Company Building and the Milam Street Auto Row." OffCite, October 23, 2018. http://offcite.org.

Hlavaty, Criag. "Former Houston Press Building in Downtown Houston to Be Demolished." *Houston Chronicle*, September 13, 2018. https://www.chron.com.

Houston public media staff. "Another One Bites the Dust: A Closer Look at the Shelor Building Demolition." *Houston Chronicle*. December 12, 2018. https://www.houstonpublicmedia.org.

Howard, Joy. "Market Square Historic District." Houston.com: A City Guide, 2007. http://www.houston.com (site discontinued).

Kleiner, D.J. "Allen's Landing." *Handbook of Texas Online*. Texas State Historical Association, June 15, 2017. https://tshaonline.org.

Koush, Ben. "Two Hotel Rehabs Illustrate Evolving Attitudes About Preservation in Houston." *Architect's Newspaper*, September 20, 2016. https://archpaper.com.

Ledoux, Abby. "Farewell to the '20s-Era Former Houston Press Building." *Houstonia*, September 13, 2018. https://www.houstoniamag.com.

Ornish, Natalie. "Gordon Jewelry Corporation." *Handbook of Texas Online*. Texas State Historical Association, June 15, 2010. https://tshaonline.org.

Pease, S.W. "Stowers, George Arthur." *Handbook of Texas Online*. Texas State Historical Association, June 15, 2010. https://tshaonline.org.

Post Properties. "The Historic Rice Hotel, Shuttered for 20 Years, Again a Houston Landmark." Hotel Online, October 1998. http://www.hotel-online.com.

Preservation Houston. "Harris County Courthouse." Preservation Progress, 2007. http://ghpa.org (site discontinued).

———. "Humble Tower." Preservation Progress, 2007. http://ghpa.org (site discontinued).

———. "Merchant and Manufacturers (M&M) Building. Houston Deco." Preservation Progress, 2007. http://ghpa.org (site discontinued).

———. "National Biscuit Co. Building." Preservation Progress, 2007. http://ghpa.org (site discontinued).

———. "Past Good Brick Award Recipients." Preservation Progress, 2018. http://ghpa.org (site discontinued).

———. "Plaza Hotel." Preservation Progress, 2007. http://ghpa.org (site discontinued).

———. "Post-Dispatch Building." Preservation Progress, 2007. http://ghpa.org (site discontinued).

———. "Texas State Hotel." Preservation Progress, 2007. http://ghpa.org (site discontinued).

Sarnoff, Nancy. "Updates Planned for Historic Downtown Rice Building." *Houston Chronicle*, October 10, 2014. http://www.houstonchronicle.com.

Welling, David. "The Picture Palaces: 1923 Majestic." Cinema Houston, 2016. http://www.cinemahouston.info (site discontinued).

Williams, Amelia W. "Allen, Augustus Chapman." *Handbook of Texas Online*. Texas State Historical Association, June 9, 2010. https://tshaonline.org.

Miscellaneous

Chapman, Betty T. Houston's Historic Oil Buildings. Houston Preservation.

Preservation Services, City of Houston Department and Planning. Warehouse District, Houston, Harris County. Historic Resources Inventory, August 31, 1991.

United States Bureau of Prisons. Metropolitan Detention Center. Houston: Environmental Impact Statement, 1994.

Other Print Sources

I used the City of Houston planning and developments resources for historic preservation landmarks, as well as the Department of the Interior's resources for locations listed on the National Register of Historic Places.

BIBLIOGRAPHY

These documents provide information on the past and present of historic locations throughout Houston through applications filed for inclusion on said lists. A listing of every document used can be found at:

City of Houston Planning and Development. Landmark Designation Reports. https://www.houstontx.gov/planning/HistoricPres/landmarks.html

United States Department of the Interior. National Register of Historic Places Nomination Forms, City: Houston. https://atlas.thc.state.tx.us/

INDEX

A

Alfred Charles Finn 42
Allen, Augustus 13, 81, 98
Allen brothers 13, 16, 28, 155
Allen, John 13, 30, 98
Allen's Landing 19, 25, 30, 31, 81,
    121, 188
American Institute of Architects 67
apartments 24, 33, 34, 39, 40, 64,
    90, 101, 102, 111, 115, 146
Architecture Center Houston 67
Art Deco 25, 44, 69, 76, 101, 146,
    147, 164, 181
artist 23, 30, 33, 106, 139
Art Moderne 42, 127
Art Noveau 25
Astrodome 190
Austin, John 13, 123, 155
Austin, Stephen F. 13

B

Bailey, James 69
Baker, James A. 103, 104
bank 28, 29, 37, 42, 44, 51, 65, 67,
    69, 70, 73, 77, 78, 80, 86, 88,
    91, 92, 94, 96, 157
Baptist Hill 91
barber 53, 56, 68, 69, 127, 153
baseball 55, 142, 147
bayou 13, 16, 26, 30, 70, 73, 80,
    112, 156
Beaux-Arts 28, 65, 69, 88
boardinghouse 63, 106, 127
brewery 28, 56, 72, 80, 81, 153
bridge 26, 81, 102
Buffalo Bayou 13, 17, 26, 29, 30,
    80, 91, 112, 113, 121, 123,
    124, 146, 151, 155, 156, 159,
    179, 188
bungalow 108

C

Camp Logan 186, 187
Catholic 37, 63, 127, 128, 147
cemetery 23, 123, 128, 129, 137,
    156, 157
church 13, 37, 45, 54, 62, 63, 90,
    91, 94, 96, 108, 110, 127,
    128, 129, 131, 132, 133, 136,
    137, 145, 146, 151, 166
city hall 16, 18, 19, 88, 96, 97, 126,
    165
City of Houston Archeological and
    Historical Commission 23
Civil War 16, 26, 54, 78, 105, 129,
    137, 139, 142
Classical Revival 51, 55
coffee 37, 56, 133
Colonial 169, 176
convent 39, 40
convention 38, 84
cotton 52, 54, 57, 73, 75, 142
courthouse 13, 36, 47, 53, 57, 58
Courthouse Square 58, 105
Craftsman 123, 168

D

department store 42, 44, 60, 69, 79,
    92, 96, 147

E

East End 127, 128
Episcopal 132, 133

F

federal 19, 31, 46, 47
financial district 65, 69
Finger, Joseph 31, 69, 101
fire 23, 28, 34, 39, 40, 54, 60, 87,
    89, 90, 144, 151, 153, 158
fire department 36, 38, 165, 183
fire station 36, 117, 122, 126, 145,
    158, 165
flagship 49, 147
flood 73, 81
football 136, 139, 154, 174, 175
Freedmen's Town 91, 104, 110,
    142, 146

G

Galveston 17, 39, 42, 46, 49, 114, 121,
    126, 139, 147, 155, 188, 191
Galveston, Harrisburg, & San
    Antonio Railway 126
George Hermann 74
German 28, 104, 107, 108, 124,
    128, 157, 181
Glenwood Cemetery 27, 41, 155,
    156, 157
Gothic 34, 94, 108, 132
governor 76, 84
Grand Central Depot 163
Grand Central Station 24
Great Depression 18, 51, 97, 100
Greater Houston Preservation
    Alliance 11, 19, 37
Great Southwest Life 50
Greek Revival 60, 62, 67, 105,
    107, 110
grocery 53, 75, 114, 164

H

haberdashery 56, 79
Hare and Hare 176, 186
Harris County 16, 32, 36, 40, 47,
    60, 62, 75, 103, 108, 109,
    112, 113, 126, 128, 136, 188
Harris County Courthouse 16, 58,
    62, 63
Hedrick and Gottlieb 77
Herald Park 147
Heritage Society 11, 103, 104, 106,
    109, 110
Hermann, George 96, 183
HISD 140
historic district 81, 121, 123
Hogg 76
hospital 23, 39, 40, 91, 135, 136
hotel 24, 31, 38, 46, 47, 49, 50, 51,
    53, 56, 62, 63, 82, 84, 88, 98,
    101, 113, 122, 143
Hotel Row 56
Houston and Texas Central
    Railway 14, 24, 113
Houston Astros 55, 190
Houston Belt and Terminal
    Railway 54, 62, 124, 126
Houston Buffaloes 142, 147
Houston Chronicle 47
Houston College for Negroes 136,
    140
Houston Colored Junior College
    136, 137, 140
Houston Community College 132
Houston East and West Texas
    Railway 86
Houston Heights 163, 164, 165
Houston Heights Association 164,
    165

Houston Independent School District
    132, 139, 140, 154, 181
Houston Junior College 139, 140
Houston Livestock Show and
    Rodeo 191
Houston Oilers 175, 190
Houston Post 47, 51
Houston Public Library 106, 166
Houston Riot 137
Houston Rockets 190
Houston, Sam 13, 56, 97, 183
Houston Ship Channel 16, 52,
    112, 126
Hughes, Howard 148, 157
Hunt, Jarvis 85

I

Incarnate Word 39, 40
International style 45
Irish 151
Italianate 68, 80, 82, 85, 87, 88
Italian Renaissance 73, 93, 98
Italian Renaissance Revival 37

J

Jewish 132, 151
Johnson Space Center 189
Jones, Jesse 17, 38, 56, 73, 82, 101
Juneteenth 139

K

Kennedy, John 78, 89, 129
Kirby, John Henry 44
Kress 48, 49

L

library 91, 97, 100, 166
Lloyd and Morgan 45
lofts 23, 29, 44, 49, 50, 69, 75, 77, 84, 85
LULAC 84, 143

M

Magnolia Brewing 72
Magnolia Park 126, 127
market house 16
Market Square 16, 17, 18, 19, 81, 88, 97, 123, 129
marquee 44
Mason 42
Mauran, Russell, and Crowell 17
MD Anderson 53
memorial 41, 167
Memorial Hermann Hospital 75
mercantile 101
Methodist 94, 136, 137, 145
Midtown 18, 131, 144
Mission 40
Moderne 132
movie theater 86
mural 68, 91, 98, 128
museum 140, 145, 148, 178, 179, 184, 191
Museum District 26, 131, 181

N

NAACP 91
NASA 84, 189, 190, 191
National Historic Landmark 189

National Register of Historic Places 12, 81, 155, 164, 165, 168, 179, 191, 198
Neoclassical 51, 58, 75, 86, 157
1900 hurricane 46
NRG Park 26

O

oil 42, 46, 47, 51, 57, 77, 96, 98
Omaha and South Texas Land Company 163, 167, 168

P

Palais Royal 44, 92
park 28, 31, 39, 55, 74, 81, 97, 102, 105, 106, 110, 137, 139, 140, 159, 163, 167, 181, 185, 186, 187
Pillot 60, 62, 75, 107, 114
police department 36, 187
Port of Houston 17, 188
post office 28, 46, 47
Preservation Houston 19, 75
Preservation Texas 37
Produce Row 65, 66, 70, 121
Prohibition 69, 72, 81

Q

Quality Hill 14, 17, 62, 63, 64
Queen Anne 64, 123, 168, 179

R

railroad 72, 73, 85
Renaissance Revival 89, 100

Republic of Texas 13, 58, 75, 81, 82, 157, 181
Rice Institute 73, 84, 172
Rice University 26, 65, 73, 84, 147, 171, 174
Rice, William Marsh 73, 82, 106, 171
River Oaks 8, 33, 176
Romanesque 63, 127, 145
Romanesque Revival 31, 112

S

Sam Houston Park 19, 102, 103, 104, 107, 108, 109, 183
Sanguinet and Staats 29, 51, 92
school 37, 134, 136, 139, 154, 181
segregation 130, 140, 154
Sisters of the Incarnate Word 90
skyscraper 45, 46, 50, 57, 65, 86, 88, 92, 93, 94, 96
slaves 23
slipcover 45, 47, 86, 92
SMOM 127
South End 33
Southern Pacific 24, 72, 73, 85, 113, 192
South Texas College of Law 101
South Texas Junior College 25
Spanish 38, 40, 76, 84, 115, 128, 146
Spanish Colonial 86, 94, 136
stadium 190
Staub, John 178, 179
Sterling, Ross 51, 57, 77, 98
streetcar 53

T

Taylor, James Knox 46

telephone 35, 49
temple 42, 132
Texaco 39, 46, 50, 94
Texas and New Orleans Railway 85
Texas Company 39
Texas Federal style 66
Texas Historical Commission 11, 47
Texas Historic Landmark 146
Texas Medical Center 26, 40, 53, 130, 181
Texas Southern University 91, 136, 140, 141
theater 44, 47, 56, 73, 84, 164, 177, 180, 183
Tudor 68, 176
tunnel 91, 93

U

undertaker 53
Union Pacific 85
Union Station 18, 53, 54, 55, 56, 130
United States Army 101
University of Houston 25, 113, 139, 140, 175

V

Victorian 32, 41, 62, 70, 75, 81, 86, 87, 102, 109, 130, 155, 167, 168
Vinegar Hill 24, 155

W

warehouse 33, 34, 35, 57, 66, 68, 70, 111, 112, 113, 114, 115, 159
Washington Avenue 155, 156, 157, 158, 159

Watkin, William Ward 84
West End Park 142
Western Union 35, 65, 73
Westheimer 53
White Oak Bayou 13, 108, 112,
    121, 151, 163
World War I 18
World War II 34, 42, 49, 115, 130,
    167

Y

Yates, Jack 91, 110, 139
yellow fever 23, 39, 129

Z

zoo 102, 183, 184

ABOUT THE AUTHOR

T ristan Smith is an independent historian living in the suburbs of Houston, Texas, with his family. For more than twenty years, he has worked for museums and nonprofits in Kansas, Missouri and Texas in marketing, curatorial, education, volunteer, management and administrative capacities. Museums he's been involved with have featured natural history, the 1950s, fine art, community history, a sunken steamboat found in a Kansas cornfield, a United States president and fire history. He has also consulted organizations and municipalities in historic preservation. He is the author of *Images of America: Houston Fire Department*, published by Arcadia Publishing in 2015.